Broadway's
Most Wanted

Broadway's Most Wanted

The Top 10 Book of Dynamic Divas,
Surefire Showstoppers,
and Box Office Busts

Tom Shea

Brassey's, Inc.

WASHINGTON, D.C.

Library of Congress Cataloging-in-Publication Data

Shea, Tom, 1966–
    Broadway's most wanted : the top 10 book of
dynamic divas, surefire showstoppers, and box
office busts / Tom Shea.—1st ed.
        p.   cm.
    Includes index.
    ISBN 1-57488-596-0 (alk. paper)
    1. Musicals—History and criticism.   2. Musical
theater—History and criticism.   I. Title.
ML2054.S44 2004
782.1′4—dc22   2003028039

Printed in Canada on acid-free paper
that meets the American National Standards
Institute Z39-48 Standard.

Brassey's, Inc.
22841 Quicksilver Drive
Dulles, Virginia 20166

First Edition

10   9   8   7   6   5   4   3   2   1

Contents

Contents

Illustrations

Preface

This is my first book, and trust me, it's no day at the beach writing one, even when it's a subject as close to the heart as musicals are to my heart. (For the record, I do live near the beach, but sand gets in your computer, so I don't recommend writing there.) No one who creates does so alone, and there are many people I have to acknowledge for their direct and indirect assistance in the creation of *Broadway's Most Wanted*.

First of all, my editor, Don Jacobs, at Brassey's. Thanks for the opportunity and all your help. Don McKeon at Brassey's was also of great help to me. My brother, Stuart Shea, was my road grader and not only gave me the idea for writing this book; his assistance in its assembly has been invaluable and much appreciated. I urge you all to pick up his book in this series, *Rock and Roll's Most Wanted*. Thanks, Stu. You'll never know what it's meant. My friends and colleagues Lara Teeter, Neda Spears, Francesca Peppiatt, Meghan Falica, Emir Yonzon, and Diane van Lente provided materials invaluable to the production of this book as well, and for that, they have my best thanks.

Personally, I would like to acknowledge the talented tap dance team of Mandelbaum, Mordden, Filichia, Gottfried, Green, Guernsey, and Suskin for their inspiration. The folks at Chicago's Navy Pier, Light Opera Works in Evanston, Illinois, and the folks at Porchlight Music Theater, Bailiwick Repertory, and City Lit Theater in Chicago kept me sane (and working) during the writing of this book. If you live in or around Chicago, see something at each of these theaters right now. To my friends Jeanne Arrigo, Gretchen Wilhelm, Michael Kotze, David Hoth, Rebecka Reeve, Julie Boesch, Shaun O'Keefe, Henry Odum, Kara Chandler, James Pelton, Don Shell, Page Hearn, Doug MacKechnie, David Breslow, Denise McGowan, Mary Lou Doherty, George Light, and Cecilia Garibay, my love and thanks. To my sweet Macheath, who couldn't be less like his namesake, I love you. To Richard P. Hoffman, Michael and Candace Pufall, Sandi Phillips, Sandra Franck, Philip Kraus, and Hub Owen, for auld lang syne. To absent friends, I can only send you my love and everlasting thoughts. My family has always been behind me, Stu, Ceci, John, and especially Mom and Dad. *Saecula Saeculorum.*

Finally, to those who make the musical theater, the writers, actors, choreographers, scenic artists, tech folk, stage managers, producers, and audiences: You make my world better with your efforts, and this book is for you.

I only hope it's worthy.

Introduction

I guess it was Gilbert and Sullivan that started it all. My parents both appreciated the genius of the English duo, whose deceptively lighthearted comic operas set the tone for everything that was to follow in the musical theater. That appreciation rubbed off on my brothers and me very, very early, and soon enough, cast albums of *West Side Story*, *Oklahoma!*, and even *Sweeney Todd* came home from the library. Pretty soon, my whole family was indulging the habit, buying not only *Finian's Rainbow*, but *Greenwillow*, *Candide*, and *Follies in Concert* as well. I was hooked.

Okay, if any or all of the above makes no sense to you, Toothsome Reader, fret not. It's just my way of saying I love the musical theater and have for a long time. It's a unique art form, which, like all great art forms, has evolved (some would say *de*volved, given the current state of the art) over time, changing as the times have demanded.

Broadway's Most Wanted is a book to honor the creators, performers, and audiences who have made the musical theater what it is today: the good, the bad, and the really, really ugly. When a show is a hit, the world is a wonderful place. But most show freaks will tell you that a bomb of a show, and I mean a real turkey, is as precious and enjoyable, in its own perverse way, as a hit. So you'll find lists of The Bad and The Ugly as well as lists of The Good. It's all so much fun, anyway.

Let's get this out of the way right off: Broadway. For the purposes of this book, we use the term "Broadway" loosely, and not literally (i.e., the legitimate New York playhouses located between the low Forties and low Sixties on Manhattan Island in New York City). Think of it as the catchall to define all of musical theater. Broadway is obviously much more than musicals, and vice versa, but there you go. To limit the scope of this book to only those shows that have played Broadway would be to exclude, which is something as a writer (and, indeed, as a performer) I can't abide. So you'll find references to off-Broadway (like the all-time long-running champ, *The Fantasticks*), regional theaters across the country (like *Casper, the Musical* and *Sylvia's Real Good Advice*), and musicals from abroad (like *Chess* and *The Beautiful Game*).

A few terms with which the novice may not be familiar: A musical, on paper, consists of **music, lyrics** (the rhyming text accompanying the music), which together constitute the **score** of a musical, and a **libretto** (the **script**), also called the **book**. The **scenic, costume**, and **lighting designers**, in addition to the **music director** and the **choreographer**, who invents the dances for the musical, are under the aegis of the **stage director**, who in turn collaborates with all and reports to the **producer** of the musical, all in the effort to create the best **show** possible. A show **rehearses**, then, after a **preview period** in which one hopes problems are ironed out in front of an audience, **goes up** (opens) on a predetermined date. Then after critics review the show, all and sundry can practice their **Tony Award speeches**. Or, they can get bad reviews and **close** in a week, adding yet one more title to the list of **flops** to plague Broadway.

That's basically what happens to a musical. This book will introduce you to various lists of musicals, some fun, some serious, some famous, and some obscure. I hope you'll be as intrigued as I was the first time I heard a piece of musical theater. If that's the case, or even if it's not, just do what I do, and what the Victorians did: Blame it on Gilbert and Sullivan.

I'm the Greatest Individual

10 Notable Tony Winners

The American Theater Wing's Antoinette Perry Award, shortened in pop-culture parlance to the Tony Awards, are Broadway's supreme achievement and honor. Here are ten notable winning examples of "distinguished achievement in the theater."

1. HAROLD PRINCE

Harold Prince, the innovative director and producer, is the proud possessor of a staggering 20, count 'em, 20 Tony Awards—more than any other individual. Prince's Tony tally includes one special award for career achievement, eight for producing (starting in 1955 with *The Pajama Game*), and eight for directing (his last was for the revival of *Show Boat* in 1995). He often combined directing and producing, and came up Yahtzee, most notably for his shows with Stephen Sondheim in the 1970s: *Company, Follies, A Little Night Music,* and *Sweeney Todd, the Demon Barber of Fleet Street.*

2. *THE PRODUCERS*

Mel Brooks's riotous musical farce from 2001 is the Broadway show with more Tony Awards than any other. *The Producers*, based on Brooks's film of the same name, enjoyed some great buzz when it previewed in Chicago, and there was no stopping it by the time it hit New York. The show is an overstuffed, laff-a-minnit, anything-goes, old-fashioned musical comedy, the likes of which hadn't been seen on Broadway in years. It was no surprise when the raves and massive lines at the box office prompted Tony voters to reward the show with an unprecedented 15 nominations. So great was the sweep on awards night that the show won for every category in which it was nominated. Its only losses belonging to three actors (Roger Bart, Brad Oscar, and Matthew Broderick) nominated against other *Producers* cast members. By the end of the night, *The Producers* had racked up twelve Tonys.

3. STEPHEN SONDHEIM

The greatest composer-lyricist of his generation, Stephen Sondheim is the proud and rightful owner of six Tony Awards (should be nine, but who's counting? Well, I am. Ahem: *A Funny Thing Happened on the Way to the Forum*, *Pacific Overtures*, *Sunday in the Park With George*. Discuss.) for his thrilling and inventive scores for *Company*, *Follies*, *A Little Night Music*, *Sweeney Todd*, *Into the Woods*, and *Passion*. The first three shows on the list gave Sondheim a unique Tony three-peat for the composer and lyricist awards. Tony voters and theater fans alike await his next Broadway musical (hopefully the long-delayed *Bounce*) like a message from Olympus. Unhappily for all, it's nine years and counting.

4. *HELLO, DOLLY!*

Before *The Producers* did its Tony smash-and-grab, there was *Hello, Dolly!* The breezy, brassy Jerry Herman-Michael Stewart musical about everyone's favorite pushy matchmaker held the record for the most Tony Awards for 27 years. The troubled David Merrick production just barely managed to scrape together its opening night, but it was obviously top-drawer musical theater from the get-go. The press quickly labeled *Hello, Dolly!* a smash, and its hot-ticket status smoothed the way to its winning an then-unprecedented 10 Tony Awards.

5. ANGELA LANSBURY/GWEN VERDON

Two of the greatest Broadway performers in history share the most Best Musical Actress Tony Awards. Gwen Verdon, aka Sex on a Stage, the adorable red-haired triple threat and muse of Bob Fosse, won for her sensuous Lola in *Damn Yankees*, her sensusous scene-stealing in *Can-Can*, her sensuous Anna Christie in *New Girl in Town*, and her sensuous redheadedness in *Redhead*. Also the owner of four Tonys is the woman who's basically Verdon's stage alter ego, Angela Lansbury. The elegant and hilarious character actress won for her Rose in the 1974 revival of *Gypsy*, her Madwoman of Chaillot in *Dear World*, her indelible many-costumed *Mame*, and for her perfect Cockney capitalist, Mrs. Lovett, in *Sweeney Todd*.

6. FRANKIE MICHAELS

Frankie Michaels won the Tony for Best Featured Actor in a Musical in 1966 for his performance as young Patrick Dennis in *Mame*. He was also ten years old when it happened, making him the youngest Tony recipient ever. Young Master Michaels never won another Tony and never acted in another show on Broadway. He had had some mild success as a child actor on television before *Mame*, but his performance in that show, and his place in the Tony history books, are all that theater fans need to remember him.

7. DAISY EAGAN

Eleven-year-old Daisy Eagan became the youngest female performer to win a Tony for her portrayal of Mary Lennox, the juvenile heroine of *The Secret Garden*. Her unsympathetic and proactive performance earned her raves and, on Tony night, a medallion and a kiss on the head from Audrey Hepburn. Eagan then proceeded to give the most adorable acceptance speech in Tony history (or at least since Debbie Shapiro's "My husband told me not to dither" speech in 1989), calling out to her mom and dad who seemed to be in the balcony of the Minskoff Theater. Unlike many child performers, who have trouble fulfilling their early promise, Eagan seems remarkably well-adjusted. Even though she has appeared on Broadway only once since *The Secret Garden*, in *James Joyce's The Dead* in 2000, she was featured on Bravo network's reality series *The "It" Factor*, which followed young actors around the city on auditions, etc. She appears sporadically in theater now and maintains a healthy Internet presence, free of artifice and "child star" posing.

8. BOB FOSSE

Broadway's sexy older brother, Bob Fosse, was one of the greatest director-choreographers in Broadway history. He also was the recipient of nine Tony Awards, for projects as diverse as the state-of-the-art hoofing for *The Pajama Game* and *Damn Yankees*, his bizarre but brilliant melding of vaudeville, commedia dell'arte, and strippin' in *Pippin*, and his stubborn refusal to throw the kitchen sink into his *Dancin'*. Fosse's early success on shows like *Damn Yankees* and *Redhead* assured him a place among the leading lights, and this place begat a new, and some would say imperial, way of creating shows, as epitomized by his near-total artistic control over shows like *Pippin* and *Chicago*. But nine Tonys will earn you that kind of control.

9. OLIVER SMITH

A winner of seven Tony Awards for scenic design, Oliver Smith designed sets for more than 125 shows in a career that spanned over 50 years. His Tony-winning musical designs are a trip through the history of musical theater in America: *Camelot*, *My Fair Lady*, *West Side Story*, *Baker Street*, *Hello, Dolly!*, *The Sound of Music*. And if the Tonys had existed in 1944, he surely would have won for his awesome sets for *On the Town*. Smith's career as codirector and designer of Ballet Theater (later the American Ballet Theater) led to his designing and producing for Broadway. No designer has been more honored, or perhaps more influential.

10. TOMMY TUNE

Tommy Tune shares a Tony record with Harvey Fierstein (but two of Fierstein's awards are for plays, not musicals—so maybe next book, Harvey): Tonys in four separate creative categories (excluding Producer credits). The supremely gifted and Texas-tall Tune started out as a hoofer (one critic called him the tallest chorus dancer he'd ever seen) and, in 1973, won a Featured Actor Tony for his work in *Seesaw*, iced by his very own number, "It's Not Where You Start." He won his first Tony for director of a musical in 1982, for his sensational staging of *Nine*, besting his friend and mentor, Michael Bennett. The next season, he won his Tony as a lead actor, and shared the choreography prize with Thommie Walsh, for *My One and Only*. Tune has won two prizes each for director and choreographer since: in 1990 for his amazing *Grand Hotel: The Musical* and, the next year, for his work on *The Will Rogers Follies*.

With Their Awful Clothes and Their Rock-and-Roll

10 Musicals Written by Famous Rock Artists

B ack in 1968, a revolution swept through the musical theater when *Hair*, the first true rock musical, ushered in a change that shook Broadway to its foundations and is still being felt today! Nope, sorry, *just kidding*. Most rock musicals were too disposable and untheatrical to carry enough weight to last, but here are ten shows whose composers know at least a thing or two about the rock game.

1. *CHESS* (BENNY ANDERSSON/ BJORN UJLVAEUS)

Benny Andersson and Bjorn Ujlvaeus are better known as the B-for-brain-trust of the Swedish pop leviathan ABBA. *Chess*, written originally in 1985 and released as a pop album (which yielded the songwriters yet another top-10 hit, "One Night in Bangkok") became a stage musical in 1986.

Chess is about a love triangle formed during a US/

Russia chess match, with the board game serving as a metaphor for the Cold War. It became a smash in London, though with a new libretto, it was a surprising failure on Broadway despite a powerful cast of singers. Since its conception, *Chess* has, of course, become somewhat obsolete, and, due to its outdated politics and even more outdated synthpop, is not often performed any more.

2. *WHISTLE DOWN THE WIND* (JIM STEINMAN)

Andrew Lloyd Webber collaborated with pop composer Steinman (best known as the author of many of Meat Loaf's biggest hits) on this musical adaptation of the 1961 British film about three children who discover a murderer hiding in their barn and mistake him for Christ. Headed for a high-profile Broadway opening in 1998, the production was scuttled by mutual consent of the authors and director Harold Prince, all of whom perhaps thought the show's allegorical nature was poorly handled. Washington, DC, was the last stop for the show. The score, as heard on CD, does reassure the listener of Lloyd Webber's formidable gifts.

3. *EIGHTY DAYS* (RAY DAVIES)

The Kinks' energetic frontman wrote this musical version of Jules Verne's classic tale of English ingenuity in the early eighties, after his first musical adaptation, a version of Aristophanes' *The Poet and the Women*, which was unfortunately called *Chorus Girls*. Director Des McAnuff developed *Eighty Days* in San Diego, at LaJolla Playhouse, where it stalled on its way to Broadway.

4. *THE CAPEMAN* (PAUL SIMON)

Notorious autocrat Simon had no first-hand experience with the Broadway process and therefore was unwilling (or unable) to relinquish creative control of this moody, almost cantata-like 1998 musical tale of a murder on the *barrio* streets of New York. This creative logjam (modern-dance maven Mark Morris was to direct and choreograph; he was replaced by Jerry Zaks and Joey McKneely when the blood started flowing) was part of the failure of the show, which critics called leaden and unfocused. Simon's score, written with Derek Walcott and featuring the elegant doo-wop "Satin Summer Nights," did receive a Tony nomination.

5. *THE WHO'S TOMMY* (THE WHO)

Tommy, the quintessential rock opera, which had already been filmed successfully in 1975 with an all-star cast, was given the Broadway treatment in 1993 following several quasi-staged all-star concert presentations of the score. Director Des McAnuff gave the show, written mainly by The Who's Pete Townshend, a stronger narrative, focusing much of the action on the characters' reaction to the events of World War II and its aftermath on the splintered, dysfunctional Walker family. The dazzling, brilliantly designed, and cinematically staged production was a smash hit, though not the rebirth of the rock musical some predicted it would be.

6. *IN A PIG'S VALISE* (AUGUST DARNELL, A/K/A KID CREOLE)

Songwriter August Darnell is perhaps better known by the *nom de pop* Kid Creole, a zoot-suited wildman

fronting his band The Coconuts. In 1989, Darnell collaborated with the playwright Eric Overmyer on the off-
Broadway musical *In a Pig's Valise*, a wacky and stylish
private-eye spoof featuring a not-yet-famous Nathan
Lane. The "hardboiled yarn with music," as Lane described it to *Theater Week* magazine, played New
York's Second Stage.

7. *BIG RIVER* (ROGER MILLER)

Yet another musical directed by Des McAnuff (the *auteur*-by-right of contemporary rock musicals, it would
seem) and developed in La Jolla, California, and at the
American Repertory Theater in Cambridge, Massachu-
setts, prior to opening on Broadway in April 1985, *Big
River* took on no less a Herculean task than Mark
Twain's *The Adventures of Huckleberry Finn*.

Playwright William Hauptmann pruned Twain to fit
the stage, keeping Huck as the narrator as well as a
participant in the adventures. Folk-rock troubador
Roger Miller wrote the score, delivering a simple, pleasing treatment of Twain's novel largely devoid of his
"can't roller skate through a buffalo herd" smart-aleck-
ness. The ballad "River in the Rain" and the country-
waltz "You Oughta be Here With Me" were highlights.

8. *THE NIGHT THAT MADE AMERICA FAMOUS* (HARRY CHAPIN)

In an unusually timely project in the wait-and-see arena
of Broadway musical production, singer-songwriter
Harry Chapin rushed this revue/rock show to Broadway in 1975 to capitalize on the popularity of his hit
single "Cat's in the Cradle." The song was not heard in
the show however, theater fans saw through the spectacle, and the revue had only a short run on Broad-

way. Chapin's songs, however (including some from an earlier sci-fi musical called *Zinger*), are distinctly story-like in nature, and his off-Broadway musical *Cotton Patch Gospel* (Christ's life as told by "Matt the Revenuer"—Saint Matthew—and set in rural Georgia) and the regional theater revue *Lies and Legends* are testament to the enduring popularity (and theatricality) of his songs.

q.   *THE MYSTERY OF EDWIN DROOD* (RUPERT HOLMES)

Rupert Holmes made his career as a writer, producer, and performer in Los Angeles, most notably with the number one single "Escape (the Pina Colada Song)."

Despite its easy-listening trappings, "Escape" was a song with a true narrative, so it came as no surprise when Holmes's adaptation of Charles Dickens' unfinished novel *The Mystery of Edwin Drood* opened at the Delacorte Theatre in New York's Central Park. What *was* surprising was that Holmes wrote all of it—book, score, and orchestrations—and inserted an ingenious second-act twist: he let the audience, by vote, solve the mystery every night, effectively finishing what Dickens never wrote. After a hit engagement in the Park in the summer of 1985, *The Mystery of Edwin Drood* soon moved to Broadway and became a multi-Tony-winning hit. Holmes has written two straight plays for Broadway since *Drood*: the thriller *Accomplice* and the one-man multimedia whatizit *Solitary Confinement.*

10.   *SMOKEY JOE'S CAFÉ* (JERRY LEIBER AND MIKE STOLLER)

The great songwriting team of Leiber and Stoller gave the pop music world hit after hit in the '50s and '60s. In

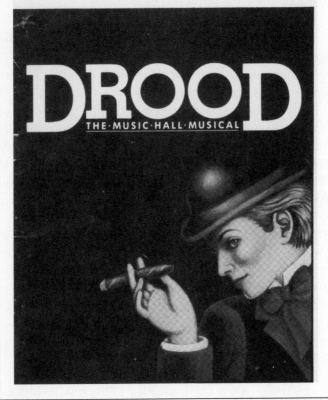

Pop songwriter Rupert Holmes made his Broadway debut in 1985 with *The Mystery of Edwin Drood,* which won five Tony Awards, two of them for Holmes.

1995, a flashy revue of their biggest hits, called *Smokey Joe's Café*, came to Broadway.

Previously produced in Chicago (under the name *That's Rock and Roll!*), director Jerry Zaks and choreographer Joey McKneely were brought in to polish up the work of the revue's creator, Otis Sallid. *Smokey Joe's Cafe* opened in the 1994–95 season, the worst Broadway season ever for new works, and lost all its seven Tony nominations. But the inventive staging, sexy advertising (featuring the short skirts and long legs of actress DeLee Lively), and familiar song titles ("Hound Dog," "I'm a Woman," "Jailhouse Rock," and, of course, "On Broadway") helped make *Smokey Joe's* one of the longest-running eligible Broadway musicals to have never won a single Tony.

I Can't Do the Sum
10 Numerical Broadway Musicals

The following ten musicals add up to much more than ten. But who's counting? Five, six, seven, eight . . .

1. **ONE, TWO, THREE, FOUR, FIVE**

This cheeky musical comedy (by Maury Yeston and Larry Gelbart) is based on the first five books of the Bible. Originally offered by Manhattan Theater Club, it was revised later as *History Loves Company* and *In the Beginning*.

2. **TWO BY TWO**

This 1970 musical based on Clifford Odets's play *The Flowering Peach*, concerning Noah and the building of his Ark, was most notable as one of Richard Rodgers's last shows, and for the return of Danny Kaye to Broadway. It was his last visit.

3. **1776**

This grand musical dealt with the drafting, debating, and signing of the Declaration of Independence during the long, hot summer of the titular year. Thanks to this Peter Stone-Sherman Edwards musical, it was indeed a very good year.

4. *1491*

This was not such a great year. Meredith Willson's Christopher Columbus musical had the great Chita Rivera as Columbus's patron, Queen Isabella. Willson's facility with musical comedy was not well suited to the European costume trappings necessary for *1491*, and the show never made it to Broadway.

5. *FIVE GUYS NAMED MOE*

A sad sack named Nomax gets advice on life and love from five fellows named Moe (Big Moe, Little Moe, Four-Eyed Moe, Eat Moe, and No Moe) in this high-spirited tribute to swing composer Louis Jordan, conceived by Clarke Peters. A big hit in London, it was less potent in the States.

6. *HALF A SIXPENCE*

Give the boy a banjo! British boy singer Tommy Steele's big splash on Broadway was *Half a Sixpence*, a Brit hit of a Cockney fable about a "workin' lad 'o inherits a bleedin' for-choon." Song-and-dance man Steele and choreographer Onna White got the best reviews.

7. *70, GIRLS, 70*

John Kander and Fred Ebb wrote this musical (with Norman L. Martin), very loosely based on the British film *Make Mine Mink*. The residents of a retirement home decide to rob a furrier, apparently just to prove they're not too old to rob a furrier. The whole enterprise was too cutesy-poo to cut very deeply at all.

8. *42nd STREET*

One of the most effective film-to-stage musical transfers, *42nd Street* was a straightforward retelling of the corny backstage film of the same name. Many, many people came to meet those dancing feet hoofing their way through Gower Champion's classic dances. (The original 1981 production didn't play at a theater on 42nd Street, though the 2002 revival did.)

9. *NINE*

The imaginative 1981 Tony winner, based on Fellini's film *8 1/2*. Tommy Tune's inventive staging and brilliant color shadings heightened the tale of a once-great film director in crisis with his art and with the women in his life.

10. *TENDERLOIN*

Tenderloin has a highly enjoyable score (by Jerry Bock and Sheldon Harnick) and is based on a true story. It concerns the Reverend Brock, a Gay Nineties holy roller intent on cleaning up the Tenderloin, New York's seedy downtown sin district. The fact that the Reverend Brock was less appealing than the media figures and skin traders he was fighting is the main reason this show flopped.

next Stop, neverland
10 Musicals Set in Imaginary Locations

Where do you long to be? Away from the humdrum? These ten musicals will indulge your fantasy quotient.

1. *GREENWILLOW*

This quaint musical from 1960 was based on a novel by B.J. Chute, who set his tale in Greenwillow, a mythical village where the male members of the Briggs family were apt to follow the "call to wander." Remarking on the elusiveness of the eponymous village, Chute himself said of Greenwillow's location, "I have been told variously that it is located in such diverse regions as Vermont, Corsica, Denmark, and the Kentucky mountains."

Broadway legend Frank Loesser (*Guys and Dolls, How to Succeed in Business Without Really Trying*) wrote the score, which is easily his most bucolic. Musical theatre neophyte (and later Oscar-winner for *The Sting*) George Roy Hill was the director, and Anthony Perkins was the star.

2. *Finian's Rainbow*

One of Broadway's most glorious scores comes from one of its most satirical musicals. Set in Rainbow Valley in the state of Missitucky, the 1947 *Finian's Rainbow* is a political satire about a corrupt senator who clashes with the tobacco sharecroppers of the valley.

The sharecroppers are spearheaded by the daughter of Finian McLonergan, an Irishman who has stolen a pot of gold from a leprechaun back in Ireland in order to plant it next to Fort Knox, where it will grow bigger. Considered wildly liberal in its time, the show gave us standards like "Look to the Rainbow," "Old Devil Moon," and "How are Things in Glocca Morra?"

3. *Shangri-La*

Between the classic 1937 Frank Capra film *Lost Horizon* and the 1973 dud remake came this 1956 stage version of James Hilton's novel of a Himalayan paradise. The premise was much the same as the film: Travelers searching for Paradise find the real thing in Tibet.

But convincingly showing Shangri-La on stage (where the mountains were clearly made of plastic), confining it to the proscenium, was harder than showing it on film, and the inevitable comparison to the movie ensured the musical would flop. Shows like this prove the rule that fantasies and special effects are better done by the movies.

4. *Li'l Abner*

Al Capp's classic comic strip seemed to cry out for musicalization and got it in this superb 1956 stage version. All the denizens of Dogpatch were there, notably Stubby Kaye as Marryin' Sam and Julie Newmar, who stopped the show (and the hearts of more than a few tired businessmen) as Stupefyin' Jones.

The score was by Gene DePaul and Johnny Mercer, with superb and very physical choreography by the great Michael Kidd. His "Sadie Hawkins' Day Ballet," in which winsome Daisy Mae and evil Appassionata Von Climax vie for the heart and mind of our hero, Abner Yokum, is considered a classic.

5. *HOT SPOT*

The great Judy Holliday gave a legendary performance as Ella, the Susanswerphone girl, in *Bells Are Ringing,* but her next show, *Hot Spot,* which never opened on Broadway, unfortunately left the comedienne high and dry. She again played a nice girl who gets mixed up in someone else's problems, this time as a Peace Corps emissary to the tiny island of D'Hum. That the name of the island was pronounced "dumb" all night gives an indication of what kind of show this was. Holliday was in financial straits at the time (1960) and only took the show to pay debts. Sadly, she died soon after it closed out of town.

6. *FLAHOOLEY*

What's a Flahooley, you ask? Well, the show's authors (E.Y. Harburg of *Finian's Rainbow*, Sammy Fain, and Fred Saidy) said it was the only word they could think of that you couldn't spell backwards. (It's really an Irish word describing a flight of fancy.)

That was the mindset behind this certifiably crazy musical, set mostly in Capsulanti, USA, at a toy factory where a young toymaker, with the help of a genie from a lamp (don't ask), creates his new doll, the Flahooley, which laughs when you shake it. The genie floods the market with Flahooleys (he doesn't want to return to the lamp), causing a depression, and the public outcry is palpable.

A 1951 Korean-War-era satire on postwar business and political ethos, *Flahooley* never found an audience on Broadway, despite the presence of such pros as Barbara Cook, Ernest Truex, and the mysterious Yma Sumac as an Arab princess with a penchant for throat singing. But *Flahooley* has charm and wit in abundance (the opening number is called, with tongue firmly in cheek, "You Too Can Be a Puppet," in which the toy-makers of Capsulanti urge America to "Come out of the woodwork, brother/And join the Brotherwood of Man."), as well as that sharp satirical edge.

7. *Via Galactica*

"Someday: The earth will be perfect. Humans will be beautiful and all the same color. And making love will be easier than making friends." So said the ad copy for *Via Galactica*, a 1972 outer-space musical with a space-age flavor. A rock musical set in outer space seemed like a groovy idea at the time, but despite the efforts of distinguished Shakespearean director Peter Hall and a talented cast, *Via Galactica* just seemed silly when actually staged.

Trampolines dotted the stage of the new Uris The-atre, so the actors bounced around. Those actors who didn't either tended to move around in cheesy space-ships (again, better done by the flicks) or on wires. Galt MacDermot wrote the score, which, along with his score for the horrific road musical *Dude*, was his sec-ond disaster of the season. These two bombs were greatly responsible for hastening the demise of the rock musical.

8. *INTO THE WOODS*

Stephen Sondheim and James Lapine's moving musical about the inner lives and dreams of fairy tale characters came to Broadway in the fall of 1987 with one of the strongest casts ever assembled for a musical (and the boot of a giant descending from the roof of the Martin Beck Theater).

The authors examined the lives of Red Riding Hood, Jack (and his beanstalk), Cinderella, and their cohorts to find out what came of their wishes and wants. The characters (plus those of a fairy tale Lapine invented, "The Baker and his Wife") all have needs, and to get what they need, they have to scheme, lie, cheat, etc., in Act One. Act Two sets the consequences of their actions in motion, *after* Happily Ever After, forcing these fairy tale characters to make real-life choices. Critics made note of the parallel between *Into the Woods* and psychologist Bruno Bettelheim's "The Uses of Enchantment," in which psychological problems can be examined through analysis of the Grimm's tales and situations.

9. *CELEBRATION*

After the legendary Off-Broadway success of *The Fantasticks,* composer Harvey Schmidt and lyricist-librettist Tom Jones had the means to do what they wanted in the theatre, and this very experimental 1969 Broadway show had been percolating for some time. It's an allegory of youth versus age, poverty and purity versus wealth and corruption, set on "a platform" and featuring an orphan battling against the richest man in the world for the heart of a winsome young beauty.

Celebration, with its masks, tights, and percussive

Stephen Sondheim and James Lapine's brilliant *Into the Woods* was a musical exploration of the psychology behind some of the best-known Grimm brothers' fairy tales.

score, was developed by the Messrs. Jones and Schmidt at their Portfolio Studio, a converted brownstone they purchased after two previous conventional Broadway successes, *I Do! I Do!* and *110 in the Shade.* But the show was clearly too experimental for Broadway, the seasonal and ritual trappings alienating rather than involving Broadway audiences at the close of the '60s.

10. *BRIGADOON*

This musical masterpiece is imagination personified, a loving tribute to the power of belief in the unreal. Two disillusioned post-World War II Americans, hunting in Scotland, stumble upon Brigadoon, a mystical village which, it turns out, only comes to life for one day every 100 years. One of the Americans, Tommy Albright, falls in love with a lovely lassie from the village. Problems arise when the brokenhearted suitor of another village girl threatens to leave, jeopardizing the village "miracle."

Brigadoon was perfectly realized in every way in its premiere in 1947, with a superb book and score from Alan Jay Lerner and Frederick Loewe, beautiful plaids dancing all over the superb Oliver Smith sets, and brilliant dances by legendary choreographer Agnes de Mille.

I Think It's Funny
10 Musicals Based on the Comics

Here, for your amusement, are ten full-color musicals you don't have to wait until Sunday to see.

1. *ANNIE*

The quintessential family musical, with kids (orphans even), a dog, and a rich Daddy. Oliver Warbucks is his name, and he's less sentimental than you'd think (the show's authors changed Daddy's politics to support, rather than criticize, the New Deal), as is this 1977 musical as a whole. Many believed this lack of schmaltz was due to the presence of the non-gooey Mike Nichols as a producer.

Whatever the reason, this superbly coordinated and performed show yielded the standard "Tomorrow," which is actually a pretty good pastiche of a Depression-era anthem, despite your niece singing it all the time. Harold Gray's comic strip heroine with the blank eyes and the adorable mutt became one of Broadway's all-time smash hits.

2. *SYLVIA'S REAL GOOD ADVICE*

Nicole Hollander's comic strip *Sylvia* features a smart-aleck single woman, her daughter, and her no-good cats, who communicate with her by hand-written (paw-written?) signs. *Sylvia's Real Good Advice*, written by Hollander herself in collaboration with Steve Rashid, premiered at Madison Rep in Wisconsin and was given a commercial run at the Organic Theater in Chicago in 1990, with real live actors playing the cats. (Sounds like a novel idea. Would that work for a full evening?) *Sylvia* dispensed her advice in sketch formula in this show, which has had some regional success.

3. *YOU'RE A GOOD MAN, CHARLIE BROWN*

The whole world was watching when Charles Schulz finally animated his beloved *Peanuts* characters in the landmark 1965 television special, *A Charlie Brown Christmas*, and all eyes were off-Broadway when Clark Gesner musicalized the gang two years later. The primary difference: The TV special used Vince Guaraldi's great combo jazz score, while Gesner's score was pure theater.

Gesner's book featured short blackout sketches modeled after *Peanuts* strips themselves, as well as longer story ideas (Lucy being queen of her Queendom, Schroeder leading a quarrelsome choir rehearsal of "Home on the Range"). Gesner's score successfully captured the spirit of Schulz's wonderfully unique characters, particularly in Snoopy's joyous "Suppertime," Charlie Brown's up-and-down "The Kite," and the anthemic standard "Happiness."

4. *LI'L ABNER*

It's ironic that one of the sexiest musicals in Broadway history should spring from one of the most grotesque comic strips ever drawn. Al Capp's legendary *Li'l Abner* and its denizens of Dogpatch, USA, were lifted off the funny pages and on to the stage with Capp's topical humor and "inhoomin" characters intact. Political satire is the order of the day, as in the strip, when Dogpatch is chosen as a missile site and Abner's all-American physique is examined by government agents for quality control.

The musical was at its best (and best-looking) when it danced, thanks to the presence of Michael Kidd as director and choreographer. Also good to look at were the leads: Peter Palmer as the perfect specimen Abner Yokum, Edith Adams as the lovely Daisy Mae Scragg, and Julie Newmar, playing to type if ever type existed, as Stupefyin' Jones, stopping the menfolk dead in their tracks with her, uh, many charms.

5. *DOONESBURY*

Garry Trudeau stopped writing his comic strip *Doonesbury* for a year in order to adapt his characters for the musical stage. The 1983 result was a fairly uneven and definitely unsuccessful evening, at least on Broadway.

The main characters of *Doonesbury*, here ready to graduate and move away from Walden Commune, were there: everyman Mike, his girl J.J., hippie Zonker Harris, mellowing radical Mark Slackmeyer, no-good-nik Uncle Duke, and football hero B.D. and his girl Boopsie. Composer Elizabeth Swados, not exactly a light tunesmith, wrote the not-exactly-light-and-tuneful music to Trudeau's only-fair lyrics. The novelty of seeing these well-known comic strip characters live in 3-D faded quicker than old newsprint, and the show closed after just 104 performances.

Many felt the lack of political satire, Trudeau's strong point in his strip, doomed the show to mediocrity. Trudeau and Swados fared better with the unabashed anti-Reagan satire *Rap Master Ronnie: A Partisan Revue*, which played off-Broadway in 1984.

6. *"IT'S A BIRD . . . IT'S A PLANE . . . IT'S SUPERMAN"*

David Newman, Robert Benton, (who would later win two Oscars for *Kramer vs. Kramer*), and the talented songwriting team of Adams and Strouse (*Bye Bye Birdie*) took Siegel and Shuster's legendary Man of Steel off the DC Comics pages and put him on stage in 1966.

Jack Cassidy played Max Mencken, Clark Kent's personal and professional rival at the *Daily Planet*, and he was joined in evil by the Flying Lings, professional acrobats who hate Superman because he flies for nothing, and also by the villainous Dr. Abner Sedgwick, a Nobel prize-loser bent on revenge. Harold Prince was the producer, and, wanting to lure kids and cheapies to the theater, the show played four matinees a week with sharply cut ticket prices. Despite a few good notices, the show closed after only 129 performances.

In his book *Contradictions*, Prince opines that the show as written in 1965 would have set the style on Broadway, but in the "Batman" pop-art year of 1966, the show appeared merely to follow the trend. A hit performance by Linda Lavin as Mencken's secretary and sets by Robert Randolph, including the *coup de theatre* of having one number sung on a huge, multi-leveled set made to look like a comics page, were the most memorable things about this *Superman*. Newman and Benton later collaborated on the successful *Superman* film franchise, where Our Hero's abilities could be greater exploited through special effects.

7. *CASPER, THE MUSICAL*

In June 2001, the well-regarded Pittsburgh Civic Light Opera mounted the world premiere of *Casper, The Musical*, based on the Friendly Ghost of Harvey Comics (to say nothing of kids' TV) fame. The decidedly family-friendly show was written by Matthew Ward, Stephen Cole, and David H. Bell. Bell also directed and choreographed the show.

The less-than-genius plot has little Casper haunting a house with his nutty uncles Stretch, Stinky, and Fatso; they're set into a tizzy by reality-game show hostess Magdalena Monteverde, who uses the house for her Treasure Hunts and decides to stay. Uh-oh. Soon, with the help of the gentle Casper, all and sundry realize that the greatest treasure to be found is within. Ahhhh.

More important than the good reception *Casper* got in Pittsburgh before touring to Kansas City and Dallas was the good feeling engendered by the presence of the show's star, Chita Rivera. Looking and sounding great as always, the ultra-classy Rivera came in for the lion's share of, well, everything, because she's Chita Rivera.

8. *Snoopy!!!*

Like Bart Simpson stealing *The Simpsons* from the show's ostensible hero, Homer, Snoopy eventually eclipsed Charlie Brown as the most popular character in Charles Schulz's *Peanuts* strip. Such was Snoopy's popularity that he became the de facto mascot of America's space program and even ran for President. Following in the footsteps of his master, Snoopy became the star of his own musical.

Larry Grossman and Hal Hackady wrote the score for *Snoopy!!!*, which boasted three librettists. The show started life in San Francisco way back in 1975, finally reaching New York in the 1982–83 season. *Snoopy!!!*, like *You're a Good Man, Charlie Brown*, featured

Snoopy and the rest of the *Peanuts* gang as well as Snoopy's feathered friend, Woodstock.

Snoopy!!! was written in much the same style as well, with many short blackouts suggested by actual *Peanuts* strips, as well as longer stories with more character arc. But despite a good score (including a stand-alone ballad called "Just One Person") and the famously lovable characters, *Snoopy!!!* has had only a sliver of the success of his master's show.

9. *ANDY CAPP*

Ruddy smashers! Andy Capp, Reg Smythe's red-nosed, work-phobic cartoon yob, was given the West End treatment in 1982. *Capp*, an extremely popular strip in America as well as the UK, was first seen on-stage in Manchester, England. British actor Tom Courtenay played Capp, with Val McLane as Flo, his long-suffering missus.

Andy Capp was written by Alan Price and Trevor Peacock, and after it played in Manchester it moved to London's Aldwych Theater. The evening concerns itself with the impending nuptials of two of Andy's and Flo's mates, Elvis and Raquel, and Andy's chronic avoidance of anything labor-intensive. Not at all intended for a Broadway audience, it boasts song titles like "Good Old Legs," "Gawd, men . . . Beasts!" and "I Have a Dream." Try getting *that* title into an American musical.

10. *R. CRUMB, THE MUSICAL*

The brainchild of artist/writer/composer Michael H. Price, *R. Crumb, The Musical* is an iconoclastic celebration of iconoclastic cartoonist Robert Crumb. The musical was produced at the Hip Pocket Theater in Fort Worth, Texas, in 1995.

After Ralph Bakshi made Crumb's adult cartoon *Fritz the Cat* into a movie, Crumb was displeased with the results, so any Crumb musical was going to need his approval. Price ensured the endorsement by having an actor dress up as Crumb and shadow him through the airport, which impressed the prickly cartoonist no end. (Crumb actually played banjo with the band at the premiere, so great was his enthusiasm.)

The show itself is a mixed bag, consisting mainly of sketches of Crumb's characters bouncing off each other (and Crumb). The score is similarly weird, consisting of the early lightnin' blues Crumb holds so dear as well as contemporary dirty blues numbers by Price. None of this is particularly stage-worthy, although there is one amusing number, "Stardust Laundry and Dry Cleaning," in which a laundry bill is awkwardly set to the tune of the Parrish-Carmichael classic "Stardust."

Show Me
Behind the Scenes

For every star performer, brilliant set designer, or whiz kid director on Broadway, there are tons of other people working hard to make musical theater magic. Here are ten of those jobs, and ten who excel at them, working just outside the spotlight.

1. GODDARD LIEBERSON, RECORD PRODUCER

An accomplished musician, the late Goddard Lieberson was perhaps the man most responsible for the popularity of the original cast recording. The Columbia Broadcasting System (CBS Radio) had expanded to become Columbia Recordings, and Lieberson's love of classical music and his business acumen allowed him to eventually rise to the top.

Following World War II, Lieberson began to challenge the supremacy of Decca Records in the cast album market by aggressively pursuing a show's recording rights by buying into many shows in order to assure those rights and recording shows from the twenties and thirties which had never been given LP treatment. His recordings of must-have hits like *My Fair*

Lady and *West Side Story* for CBS insured the upper-middle-class audience these recordings needed, and their massive popularity allowed him to record many less well known shows as well. The other record labels followed suit. The industry's niche in the popular culture is, basically, due to the foresight and acumen of Goddard Lieberson.

2. AL HIRSCHFELD, CARTOONIST

The graceful, gorgeous, and hilarious pen-and-ink drawings made by caricaturist Al Hirschfeld illuminated every theatrical season (as well as the worlds of movies, TV, and music). The New York *Times* had featured his drawings since before *Show Boat*, and he was drawing right up until the very end, when he passed away, in January 2003.

In between, he had seen everything, drawn everyone who was anyone, and become not only rich and famous (*The Line King*, a documentary film about him, was made in 1996), but also entered the popular lexicon. Hirschfeld's corner of pop culture was staked in 1945, when his daughter, Nina, was born. He featured her in a drawing, as "NINA The Wonder Child," and from then on, hid "NINAs" in nearly every drawing, allowing faithful readers to find them. It's not an exaggeration to suggest that Al Hirschfeld, due to his presence in the *Times*, did as much to make mass audiences aware of Broadway as anyone else.

3. MATHILDE PINCUS, MUSIC PREPARATIONIST

Beginning in 1953, with *Wonderful Town*, Mathilde Pincus worked as a music copyist, notating by hand the music scores used by the pit orchestra and singers. By the end of her career, she had served as either copyist or preparation supervisor on over 40 Broadway shows. Working at Chelsea Music, a sort of clearinghouse for score preparation, she mentored many of the best copyists of the era and oversaw a uniform handwriting and notation style.

It's hard to imagine how important this type of consistency was before the advent of computer software programs made everyone a cubicle copyist. How important was it? So much so that the Tony Awards Committee, in 1976, voted her a special Tony "for outstanding service to the musical theater."

4. **PAUL FORD, PIANIST**

At the 1988 Tony Awards, Stephen Sondheim, accepting his award for Best Score for *Into the Woods*, thanked his orchestrator, Jonathan Tunick, and his conductor, Paul Gemignani. Then, as an afterthought, he thanked Paul Ford, and a shriek of joy went up from the audience. Who the mad screamer was we may not know, but Ford has been getting even better response to his name in recent years. Paul Ford is a rehearsal pianist.

Ford (no relation to the fine character actor of years past who shares the same name) is Sondheim's pianist of choice, a valued member of the legendary composer/lyricist's inner creative circle. The rehearsal pianist is often the first line of communication between the composer and the rest of the world, helping to shape the score as the composer and director hear it played in rehearsal. Tempos, textures, even phrasing are aided greatly by the presence of a good rehearsal pianist.

5. ROBERT THOMAS, REHEARSAL DRUMMER

The rehearsal drummer is elemental to a choreographer, helping to create rhythms that eventually serve as templates for the dances in a show. Perhaps nowhere was the need for a competent rehearsal drummer greater than for the seminal "workshop" musical, *A Chorus Line*. And *A Chorus Line*'s rehearsal drummer was Robert Thomas.

The director and choreographer of *A Chorus Line*, Michael Bennett, met Thomas when they both worked at the June Taylor Dance Studio, Bennett teaching classes, Thomas laying down drumbeats for dancers. Soon, Thomas was helping Bennett develop the patterns that served as the bare bones for the supreme choreographic achievement that was *A Chorus Line*. Bennett respected his drummer so much that, as *A Chorus Line* became a phenomenon Thomas was promoted to Musical Coordinator, serving as a liaison between Bennett and his many touring companies.

6. PETER FELLER, SCENIC SHOP OWNER

If you saw a Broadway musical in the recent past, chances are the sets and the deck (stage floor) were built by Feller Scenery Studio. The late Peter Feller's family, scenic carpenters and engineers for generations, literally have sawdust in their veins.

Peter Feller ran Feller Scenery Studio in the Bronx, and his father, Peter, was a stagehand at the Metropolitan Opera House. (His son, also Peter, owns Feller Precision, a theatrical engineering company that takes up where Feller scenery leaves off.) Master director Harold Prince talks with admiration about rehearsing *Follies* on the built set at Feller Studios, which saved countless hours of adaptation to the severe rake, or tilt, of the stage. Prince also waxed poetic about Feller's help in adapting the Broadway Theater for the revival of *Candide* in 1974: "There's no question but that we couldn't have gotten *Candide* on without Peter Feller's help," he wrote in his book *Contradictions*. Had every director working with a Feller-built set written his own book, we'd have many, many more tributes of this nature.

7.   nIKI HARRIS, DANCE CAPTAIN

The role of the Dance Captain in a musical is a slightly precarious one. The Dance Captain must maintain all the choreographer's steps and be the choreographer's last word when questions arise during the run of the show. This normally occurs while he or she is dancing in the show at the same time. So, while dancers see the Dance Captain as staff, choreographers see him or her mainly as a dancer. The Dance Captain, therefore, must command respect from both sides.

Niki Harris is Tommy Tune's Dance Captain of choice. She came on board with him on his great *A Day in Hollywood/A Night in the Ukraine* and has been with him on the line ever since, creating goodwill while maintaining some of the best-choreographed shows of recent years. The people who matter have noticed, too. The actor Walter Willison, who danced with her in *Grand Hotel*, has stated publicly, in *Theater Week* magazine, that she "has a fabulous set of gams."

8.   STEVEN ZWEIGBAUM, PRODUCTION STAGE MANAGER

The Production Stage Manager, or PSM for short, is the eyes and ears of a musical, both in rehearsal and performance. The PSM runs and times rehearsals, coordinates production and rehearsal schedules, and juggles egos, all the while maintaining a script full of technical cues that would make a military strategist weep. One of Broadway's busiest and best is Steven Zweigbaum.

Zweigbaum made his musical stage management debut with *Shenandoah* in 1975 and since then has rarely stopped working. In addition to running rehearsals and calling cues for the show when it opens (which most PSM's do a few nights a week, turning it over to assistant stage managers the other nights), Zweigbaum coordinates touring companies of several shows as well. His most recent project has been *The Producers*. That's no vacation.

9. SEYMOUR "RED" PRESS, ORCHESTRA CONTRACTOR

The job of a musical contractor is vital to the production of a musical: Fill the pit orchestra with the best players you can, see to it that they maintain a good relationship with the conductor and the actors, and make sure they get paid on time. Not as easy as it sounds. For many years, Seymour "Red" Press has been the go-to guy when musicians are needed.

Press lists over 100 New York shows to his credit, and that's likely no exaggeration: His first Broadway show as a contractor was 1978's *Ballroom*. He serves as "Musical Coordinator" as often as he contracts the players, which means producers have as much faith in him as the music men do.

10. VINCENT SARDI, RESTAURATEUR

Vincent Sardi opened his first restaurant in 1921, on West 44th Street, right in the heart of Manhattan's theater district. The family moved the restaurant to its current location, 234 West 44th, in 1927. Since then, Sardi's Restaurant has been synonymous with Broadway. From opening nights to the caricatures on the wall to the upstairs bar, Sardi's is as colorful as Broadway itself.

Vincent Sardi was a Sicilian kid from Queens who opened his restaurant in the middle of the Jazz Age, although it was never a speakeasy. His restaurant's popularity with a certain crowd of first-nighters, who all had their own tables, cemented the "Opening Night at Sardi's" tradition. He was honored at the very first Tony ceremony in 1947, and stars still ache to be caricatured and put up on the walls of this New York institution.

It's a Hell of a Town
10 Fun City Musicals

New York's legendary Main Stem, Broadway has long been the rainbow's end for musical theater, hence the not-quite omnibus title of this book. Here are ten shows devoted to that magical talisman, the city on the Hudson.

1. *WONDERFUL TOWN*

The great songwriters Leonard Bernstein (the music) and Betty Comden and Adolph Green (the words) either together or separately wrote several musical paeans to New York. These titles are a quick trip through musical greatness: *West Side Story, Bells are Ringing*, and their first show together, *On The Town.*

Wonderful Town, scored by the three, gets the nod here as an almost perfect example of the musical-comedy genre and a perfect love letter to New York. A superb adaptation of the play *My Sister Eileen, Wonderful Town* tells the story of the Sherwood sisters, bookish Ruth and gorgeous Eileen, who have journeyed east from Columbus, Ohio, to 1935 Greenwich Village in search of fame, fortune, and fellas. Written in an unheard-of five weeks, the show featured a fine score and an unmatched star performance by Rosalind Russell as would-be writer Ruth.

2.   *RAGTIME*

The show that many call the last great musical of the twentieth century, *Ragtime* is a sweeping adaptation of the E.L. Doctorow novel of the same name, and is structured similarly. Doctorow's typical epic sweep, combining ordinary people and the famous folk with which they interact, is cleverly adapted into musical form by librettist Terrence McNally, composer Stephen Flaherty, and lyricist Lynn Ahrens.

The tony, all-white suburb of New Rochelle, home to an affluent white family, is invaded by the real world, i.e., racism, humanity, inhumanity, and other people. Whites, blacks, immigrants, and their mutual experiences, creating the tapestry of Americana at the beginning of the twentieth century, are handled with superb taste and style in this grade-A adaptation.

3.   *SWEET CHARITY*

Say "Broadway author" in a word association test and nine out of ten will answer "Neil Simon." Check. And does any Broadway composer say "New York City" more than Cy Coleman? No. Check, again. So they collaborated on a musical (with the smarty-pants lyricist Dorothy Fields) and created a sweet New York cocktail (a Manhattan?) called *Sweet Charity*.

Adapted from the Fellini film *Nights of Cabiria*, Charity is a big-hearted dance-hall girl who loves neither wisely nor well. She hooks up with all manner of New York types, from a swingin' playboy to a nerdy corporate schlub. Her adventures include a downtown rave-up ("Rhythm of Life), presided over by Big Daddy Johann Sebastian Brubeck, and a parade through the city streets ("I'm a Brass Band").

4. *SATURDAY NIGHT*

Stephen Sondheim's first Broadway musical would have been *Saturday Night*, with a book by Julius J. Epstein, adapted from Epstein's play (co-written with his brother Philip) *Front Porch in Flatbush*. Unfortunately, producer Lem Ayers died in 1952, and the production stalled. Following an abortive attempt to resuscitate the show in 1959, *Saturday Night* languished in the Land of Could-Have-Been. Forty years later, New York got its first full look at *Saturday Night*, at Second Stage off-Broadway. A youthful tale of idealism and friendship, it concerns a tight knot of twenty-somethings investing in the stock market, with that crazy Brooklyn Bridge linking them to their dreams. Several fine songs, including the clever "Love's a Bond," and the Whiffenpoof-junior "It's That Kind of a Neighborhood," gave a glorious look back through the hourglass into the early career of the Promethean career of Stephen Sondheim.

5. *BIG*

Penny Marshall's hit 1987 film *Big* is a body-switch comedy about a Jersey boy who wishes he could be tall, then wakes up and finds himself in an adult's body. The basis of the film is his quest to adapt to the adult-sized world and its attendant, adult-sized problems, while he searches for a return to his old self. Nine years later, *Big* was made into a musical of the same name. The film's success, however, was not duplicated by the musical.

An outstanding, fly-on-the-wall book by Barbara Isenberg, *Making It Big*, chronicled the show's every step, from early rehearsals to post-Tony letdown. The musical seemed to ignore (or was unable to duplicate) the strong emotional pull the film had, and, like the film, its strongest moment (an extremely easy scene to musicalize) came in the famous scene at New York City toy store FAO Schwartz, in which man-boy and toy tycoon dance on the big piano on the floor, to David Shire's clever variations on "Chopsticks."

6. *GUYS AND DOLLS*

Perhaps the greatest musical ever written, the "Musical Fable of Broadway" scores on every conceivable level. A priceless adaptation of stories written by New York's chronicler supreme, Damon Runyon (who hailed from another Manhattan—Manhattan, Kansas), particularly the short story "The Idyll of Miss Sarah Brown," Frank Loesser's score is one of the greatest ever and is more than matched by the hilarious book by Jo Swerling and Abe Burrows.

Everything in this supremely coordinated musical screams "New York City." Runyon's dizzyingly colorful Broadway underworld ("Runyonland," they called the opening sequence) was fleshed out brilliantly onstage by director George S. Kaufman and choreographer Michael Kidd, from the fictional Mindy's restaurant to the sewers where Nathan Detroit's crap game rages on, to the Save-a-Soul Mission with its window looking out on Broadway itself.

7. *RENT*

Tyro songwriter Jonathan Larson added his name to the canons of theater lore when he unexpectedly died on the opening day of his musical, *Rent*, at the New York Theater Workshop off-off-Broadway. The buzz surrounding the show and the circumstances became deafening, and Larson's adaptation of Puccini's *La Bohème* became a hit downtown, then moved virtually intact to Broadway, where it won Larson the Pulitzer Prize, posthumously, and the Best Musical Tony.

Rent takes *La Bohème* and puts a decidedly postmodern, downtown spin on it: Mimi is HIV-positive, the Marcello character ("Mark") is an experimental filmmaker, landlord Benoit is a profit-hungry real estate developer, etc. The show's success is largely due to a desire to see the pseudo-hip Alphabet City life onstage. This show is one of the first in a long time to have its own set of groupies, or "Rentheads," who camp out for tickets and see as many performances as they can.

8. *LADY IN THE DARK*

This landmark 1941 show was among the first to seriously address the social and psychological problems facing women, and it was the first musical to use sessions of analysis as a plot device. Kurt Weill wrote the hauntingly brautiful music to Ira Gershwin's brilliant lyrics. Moss Hart wrote the coded, subtext-heavy libretto.

Gertrude Lawrence played Liza Elliott, high-strung editor of *Allure* magazine, in personal and professional crisis, unable to make decisions regarding her life, her loves, and her job, afraid the city will swallow her whole. Desperate, she heads to the ofice of Dr. Brooks, who analyzes her. Part of the brilliance of this show was its refusal to play to type: The ultra-glamorous Lawrence had no star entrance or flashy moments, one of her main confidants was a gay man, and all the musical sequences in the show were dream scenes which illu-minated her demons—a "Glamour Dream," a "Wed-ding Dream," and the spectacular "Circus Dream."

9. *NEIL SIMON'S THE GOODBYE GIRL*

The title is actually longer than the run of this show, which started with a fine pedigree, but somewhere went very wrong. Neil Simon adapting his very funny (and stage-smart) hit film, Tony-winning pros David (*City of Angels*) Zippel and Marvin (*A Chorus Line*) Hamlisch to score it, and Bernadette Peters and Martin Short to star as a fading Broadway hoofer and an up-and-com-ing thespian.

So. Santo Loquasto's sets were mainly interiors, and too cartoonish at that, and the book and score never rose to the occasion offered—a sexy musical comedy about two lonely people against the big back-drop of New York Show Business. Simon himself opined that the only good thing about the show was Short's performance, and Simon later rewarded Short with 1999's revival of *Little Me*, for which Short won a Tony.

10. *SWEET SMELL OF SUCCESS*

Like the great film that inspired it, 2002's *Sweet Smell of Success* was a poison-pen letter to New York City—this "Dirty Town," as lyricist Craig Carnelia called it. Marvin Hamlisch wrote the music, and John Guare adapted the cynical screenplay to the stage.

A story of ruthless ambition run amok, a young press agent is willing to do anything to anybody to curry favor with star columnist J.J. Hunsecker, who still manages to make the young man's life a living hell.

Despite a commanding, Tony-winning performance from John Lithgow as Hunsecker, *Sweet Smell* failed, probably because its film noir, wormy-Big-Apple outlook was not exactly what Broadway audiences wanted to see after 9/11.

We Shout, "Look Out, Yale!"
10 Musicals about Sports

Though not necessarily mutually inclusive (except for Show League softball), the worlds of sports and musicals have much in common: brightly-colored clothing, legions of fans who take their passion far too seriously, corporate-sponsored homes, and scantily-clad women for those not interested in the business at hand. Here are ten musicals all about sports—the athletes and the games.

1. *Damn Yankees*

The story of Joe, a middle-aged couch potato who'd sell his soul to the devil to see his Washington Senators win the pennant over those "damn Yankees," this cheery 1959 show gave the songwriting team of Richard Adler and Jerry Ross their second consecutive smash, hot on the heels of *The Pajama Game* a year earlier.

The Senators, of course, are a hapless nine (presaging Gotham's own original Mets) rejuvenated by the arrival of "Shoeless Joe From Hannibal, Mo.," the reincarnation of our old couch-bound Joe. Under the eyes of George Abbott and Bob Fosse, the Senators roared to the flag despite the presence of Ray Walston as "Mr. Applegate," old Scratch himself, and the star turn of Gwen Verdon as Lola, his first-string home-wrecker, sent by Applegate to tempt Joe to distraction.

2. *TOO MANY GIRLS*

Three Eastern lads with gridiron skills and their prep-phenom friend Manuelito (a young Desi Arnaz) journey west to Pottawottamie College in Stop Gap, New Mexico, at the behest of a rich man intent on providing bodyguards for his spoiled, beautiful daughter.

A fairly run-of-the-mill 1939 Rodgers & Hart college musical, *Too Many Girls* was best as a showcase for its young stars, notably Eddie Bracken, Van Johnson, and the aforementioned Desi Arnaz. Young Arnaz literally stopped the show during the production number "Spic and Spanish" by coming onstage in his football uniform, with his conga drum strapped to his chest, and drumming up a storm.

3. *THE BEAUTIFUL GAME*

Andrew Lloyd Webber and Ben Elton's musical from 2000 is set during the time of the Troubles in Northern Ireland. Soccer ("football" in British parlance) is the "beautiful game" in question, serving as a refuge for the young heroes from the Catholic-Protestant violence engulfing the Ulster region. The young soccer players hope that their playing skills will serve as their ticket out of the Troubles, yet they know that the tribal nature of the game they love too easily echoes the sectarian violence ripping their country, their loves, and their lives apart. *The Beautiful Game* has, of this writing, yet to play New York.

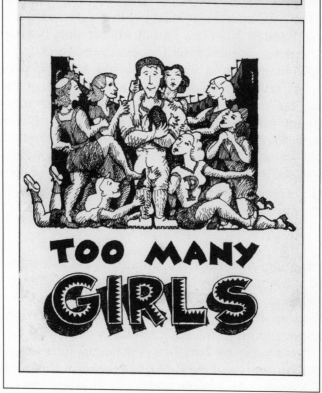

Playbill

Too Many Girls was the 1939 Rodgers and Hart musical
about college football recruits who become the big men
on campus at the apocryphal Pottawottamie University
of Stop Gap, New Mexico. Pictured is the cover of the
Equity Library Theater's 1987 revival.

4. *THE FIRST*

Musical bios about famous people don't usually work, and baseball isn't a sport easily adaptable to the stage. So a musical about Jackie Robinson breaking baseball's color barrier with the Montreal Royals and the Brooklyn Dodgers may not have been the best idea of the 1981–82 season, at least not in the pedestrian version offered in *The First*. Part of what makes biographies hard to musicalize is the believability of famous people singing, and while Robinson himself, played ably by David Alan Grier, may have been a legitimate character for musicalization, it was harder to buy Dodgers Manager Leo Durocher and team owner Branch Rickey as singing characters. The libretto for *The First* was written by ABC-TV critic Joel Seigel, which placed the broadcast and print media who covered the show in a fairly uncomfortable position: that of reviewing the work of a fellow critic.

5. *CHESS*

Another pre-sold hit from Britain, this 1986 musical used a Soviet vs. American chess masters' match as a metaphor for the Cold War diplomacy between the countries, with some star-crossed romance thrown in for those unmoved by either sports or politics.

With a score by Tim Rice (the lyricist for *Evita*, *The Lion King*, etc.) and the B-Boys of Swedish supergroup ABBA, Benny Andersson and Bjorn Ujlvaeus, the show was to be directed by the great Michael Bennett, who bought a million pounds' worth of video monitors to be used as scenic elements, effectively dwarfing a score which he saw as often unstageable. Trevor Nunn took over the direction when Bennett became ill, and it became a long-running hit in London. The show made it to Broadway, heavily revised, for a short run in 1988.

6. *annie get your gun*

One of the most popular musicals in American history, Irving Berlin's classic is set in and around the world of the rodeo—Buffalo Bill's Wild West Show, to be precise. But don't be fooled. This is no SportsCenter highlight reel. A few trick shooting scenes aside, there truly is "No Business Like Show Business," as Annie Oakley and Frank Butler spar in the center ring and woo each other behind the scenes, all the while insisting they're as wrong for each other as can be. Uh-huh.

Produced by Rodgers and Hammerstein (no dummies they) in 1946, the show was undoubtedly the best vehicle ever for the original Annie, Ethel Merman. Merman had been a leading lady for years, but Berlin's tender ballads for Annie showed the public a soft side to Merman that had never been tapped by other writers. For that reason, and despite Merman's indelible stamp on the role, every female musical-comedy star wants to play Annie Oakley at some point in her career. A revival starring Bernadette Peters hit Broadway in 1999 and found great success with everyone from Susan "Erica Kane" Lucci to country star Reba McEntire doin' what comes naturally.

7. *LITTLE JOHNNY JONES*

The first hit show by the great, proto-American songwriter, George M. Cohan, *Little Johnny Jones* was a typical turn-of -the-century Broadway show, both onstage and off. The admittedly corny, flag-waving story of a Yankee jockey in England, *Johnny* was as basic and calculated-to-please as most of the shows of the time, with little dramatic tension or story to get in the way of the girls and the socko songs.

Offstage, too, this 1904 show followed the formula of the time, all but unthinkable in today's theater economy: Open on Broadway, withdraw to the road after the inevitable bad reviews, tour the show and revise it, then hit the Main Stem again, all guns blazing. And blaze they did: Cohan's score gave us both "Yankee Doodle Boy" and "Give My Regards to Broadway," either one of which would have guaranteed Cohan's immortality and the show's success. It was revived none too successfully, however, in the early '80s, with David Cassidy not quite believable in the lead role.

8. *GOLDEN BOY*

Clifford Odets' potboiling boxing play concerns a young Italian-American palooka intent on fighting his way out of his neighborhood. Neophyte producer Hillard Elkins floated the idea of a musical version of the play to Odets, and once Sammy Davis, Jr. expressed interest, Italian Joe Bonaparte became the Negro Joe Wellington. The score was written by Lee Adams and Charles Strouse, whose previous musical, *All American*, had also been about sports, specifically college football.

The differences between play and musical turned out to be the least of the problems in getting the show on, with Odets dying in 1963 (his work was finished in 1964 by William Gibson) and the original director (and many cast members) getting lost (i.e., fired) in the shuffle. What worked, eventually, were the performance of Sammy Davis and the show's climactic fight scene, performed to percussion, and thrillingly staged in a real boxing ring by Donald McKayle.

9. *CRICKET*

Tim Rice and Andrew Lloyd Webber reunited in 1986 to write this short chamber musical about Tim Rice's favorite sport (he owns a cricket team, writes a cricket column for the London *Daily*, and has published several books on the sport). Trevor Nunn, also a cricket fan, was the director.

The piece was written as part of a Royal Command Performance for Queen Elizabeth and Prince Philip, and was also performed at Lloyd Webber's Sydmonton Festival. Due to the size and subject matter of the piece, and considering the unique circumstances surrounding its creation, it's unlikely that *Cricket* will ever be seen professionally in New York or anywhere in the States.

10. *DIAMONDS*

This off-Broadway revue from 1984 was a collection of songs and sketches about the National Pastime, directed by the legendary Harold Prince, and it featured material contributed by over 40 writers, including *Beauty and the Beast*'s Howard Ashman and Alan Menken (though writing separately) and *Cabaret*'s team of John Kander and Fred Ebb.

The upbeat, lighthearted nature of the revue made it obvious that there would be no sketches on labor disputes, no drug references, and no "Ballet of the Rainout Showing of the 1975 All-Star Game Film." About the most satirical the show got was a collection of blackout sketches taking off on voluble broadcaster Warner "Let's go to the videotape" Wolf, here impersonated by actor Chip Zien.

Again, from the Top
10 Prominent "Revisals"

T he "revisal" is a fairly new phenomenon to Broadway. A revisal is a purely commercial rethinking of
an exisiting show which is given the benefit of 20/20
hindsight and supposedly improved by wholesale
changes to songs, story, or both. Here are ten revisals
that had success at some level, either creatively or
commercially.

1. *THE PIRATES OF PENZANCE*

Gilbert and Sullivan's classic tale of duty, love, and Victorian silliness was given a full-throttle rethinking in
1980 by the New York Shakespeare Festival. New orchestrations (unfortunately overdone: listen to the xy-
lophone playing sometime!) were a good indicator of
the level of wackiness to be had.

Directed (and co-designed) by Wilford Leach, this
Pirates was an unexpected hit at the Delacorte Theater
in New York's Central Park, then moved to Broadway
for a multi-award-winning run. Incorporating two new
songs (both from the other G & S operas) and a clipper
ship's worth of physical schtick, *Pirates* never ever took

Lara Teeter

Backstage at the New York Shakespeare Festival's hit 1980
"revisal" of Gilbert and Sullivan's *The Pirates of Penzance.*
Mugging for the camera are stars (from left to right) Rex Smith,
Kevin Kline, and Tony Azito.

itself seriously. Not for the die-hard Gilbert and Sullivan
purist, perhaps, but a great deal of fun.

2. *ME AND MY GIRL*

The veddy British musical comedy *Me and My Girl* was
a smash hit between the wars in London, running for
four years in the West End and even giving birth to a
popular dance craze, the "Lambeth Walk." Richard
Armitage, the son of the show's composer, Noel Gay,
decided to remount the musical, about a Cockney
bloke who inherits a title but not the attendant snob-
bishness, in 1984, and oversaw a painstaking recon-

struction of a show largely thought to be lost to the ages. Adding three new old songs and almost completely rewriting the book, the show touched a nostalgic nerve in the West End and rode the "All Things Big and British" wave to Broadway in 1986, winning raves for the show's star, Robert Lindsay.

3. *CANDIDE*

Not only is *Candide* the Granddaddy of all flop musicals, it's also The Show That Would Not Die. After Broadway in 1956, *Candide* was tried with various and sundry revisions to script and score on tour and overseas, then greatly overhauled in 1973 for an off-Broadway production.

Hottest-director-in-the-world Harold Prince was asked to take a look at the show for the Brooklyn Academy of Music's Chelsea Theater Center. His new production was a wacky, juvenile, environmental staging with a completely new book by Hugh Wheeler and some new Stephen Sondheim lyrics to re-jiggered Leonard Bernstein melodies. The triptych-like show moved better than it had before, but it meant less. Which meant nothing to audiences, both off-Broadway and on, who responded to the show's pedigree and Prince's status and ate it up.

Prince, and especially Bernstein, kept prodding at the show, re-conceiving it for New York City Opera in 1982, Scottish Opera in 1990, Broadway *again* in 1997 after Bernstein's death, and for the Community Women's Church Guild Clock Tower Players Dinner Theater in McKeesport, Pennsylvania, in 1999.

4. *CRAZY FOR YOU*

A triumph of borrowed finery, *Crazy For You* is a 1992 musical very loosely based on a previous Gershwin brothers musical, *Girl Crazy*. *Crazy For You*, like *Girl Crazy*, concerned a man who ventured out West and fell in love with the town's only girl.

Girl Crazy later "became" *Crazy For You*, featuring a new libretto by Ken Ludwig, who added a palatable show business subplot to the proceedings. Bobby, our hero, goes to Nevada to foreclose on a theater and ends up putting on a show and falling in love. A few of the Gershwin songs from *Girl Crazy* were thrown out and other Gershwin songs ("Tonight's the Night," "What Causes That?") supported the standards from the earlier show ("Embraceable You," "I Got Rhythm"). In its spiffy new duds, *Crazy For You*, directed and choreographed in superbly physical style by Mike Ockrent and Susan Stroman, respectively, was judged to be sufficiently "new" enough to win the Best Musical Tony in 1992.

5. ***CABARET***

Cabaret, Joe Masteroff, John Kander and Fred Ebb's 1966 masterpeice of decadence unchecked, visited Broadway in 1998 in a production from London's Donmar Warehouse. While many shouted "Wilkommen" at the new production, others quietly said "A Bientôt" to the show's inherent subtext.

While the 1966 production of *Cabaret* shocked a complacent Broadway with its garish stage pictures and the adult treatment of its grim subject matter, the 1998 *Cabaret*, directed by Sam Mendes and choreographed by Rob and Kathleen Marshall, was completely and proudly vulgar while it was in the cabaret (which the audience, seated at nightclub tables, was, all night long). Not only was the show's Emcee (a thrillingly androgynous and insatiable Alan Cumming) an agent of evil in the Cabaret, but he also hovered over the show's book scenes, underscoring, with little subtlety, the impending disaster.

6. *SHOW BOAT*

America's seminal musical play, *Show Boat* suffers from a kind of schizophrenia. As the show that straddled the gap between operetta and a new kind of musical drama, *Show Boat* is often accused of being too much of one or the other, leaving purists of both art forms sharply divided on how to do justice to this masterpiece.

Show Boat has undergone countless revisions in its 75-plus year history; indeed, it's possible that there have never been two productions exactly alike on paper. Broadway's two most recent productions of *Show Boat* vividly illustrated the dichotomy inherent in the piece. Director Jack O'Brien's 1982 production was a florid, oversized, near-operatic reading of the piece, while Harold Prince's 1995 version was sleek, brilliantly streamlined, and bore striking resemblance to a contemporary musical. Tony Awards and lengthy tours followed. The one constant in both productions? The presence of actress Lonette McKee, as doomed chanteuse Julie.

7. *FLOWER DRUM SONG*

Asian-American playwright David Henry Hwang, a fierce protector of Asian-American heritage, was approached to rewrite Oscar Hammerstein's libretto to his 1958 musical (written, of course, with Richard Rodgers) *Flower Drum Song*. *Flower Drum Song*, based on Chin Y. Lee's novel, tells a fairly basic tale of assimilation versus obligation in San Francisco's Chinatown, where a young man must choose between a traditional Chinese bride and a brash, sexy Chinese-American dancer.

Hwang's new book dealt with considerable back-story and filled in the politics behind the arrival of these Chinese immigrants, and the new Broadway production (2002) altered the tunestack to fit the new story. Unfortunately, it wasn't a success in this new version, and while the show may not be tried again in either version, one might suggest not interfering with the architectural brilliance of *any* Hammerstein libretto, no matter how noble the sentiment.

8. *ANYTHING GOES*

Cole Porter wrote one of his very best scores for this 1934 shipboard farce. The first draft of the show concerned a shipwreck plot, but after the *S.S. Morro Castle* sank, the plot had to be re-written on the fly. The necessity of a quick fix introduced the world to the hugely successful writing team of Howard Lindsay and Russel Crouse, who were brought together at director Lindsay's insistence for help in patching up the book.

In 1962, *Anything Goes* was revived off-Broadway, with six other Porter songs interpolated to help prop up the typically creaky 1930s book. A brand-new version sailed into Lincoln Center in 1987, featuring four more new old songs, and a completely reworked book by John Weidman and Russel Crouse's son, Timothy. Patti LuPone's blazing performance as Reno Sweeney, evangelist-chanteuse, brought sex appeal back to the role, which had fallen into the hands of too many Jo-Anne Worleys over the years. Also noteworthy were the characters of Luke and John, "two Taiwan Chinese" named Ling and Ching in 1962, who figure in the comedy subplot and are actually somewhat empowered in the 1987 version, as opposed to being mere caricatures in 1962. Whichever version you see, the real pleasure is in hearing some of the greatest songs ever written for the theater, courtesy of one of the masters, Mr. Cole Porter.

9. *THE THREEPENNY OPERA*

Kurt Weill and Bertolt Brecht's agitprop classic first premiered on Broadway in 1933 (in an English-language version not prepared by Brecht). This bitterly political, audience-alienating *zeitoper* wasn't exactly what depression-era crowds were looking for, and it lasted only twelve performances. However, a 1954 production mounted at the Theater de Lys off-Broadway after Weill's death, and starring his widow, Lotte Lenya, was a monster hit, running for 2,611 performances.

This popular version of *Threepenny* was prepared by the gifted composer and lyricist Marc Blitzstein, who, in this version, gave the world the sobriquet "Mack the Knife" for the show's antihero, Macheath. Unfortunately, the text and political thrust of the show were considerably (albeit understandably, considering the Ike-era politics) bowdlerized.

Broadway has seen *Threepenny* twice since, most notably in a production directed by Richard Foreman in 1976. This version, translated and de-santitzed by Ralph Mannheim and John Willett, brought much of the political, scatological, and sexual energy of the piece back to the fore, and Douglas W. Schmidt's audience-alienating scenery, with its low-hung lamps and puzzlingly-placed strings criscrossing the audience's field of vision, contributing to the truly Brechtian atmosphere.

10. *IRENE*

When the idea was floated in 1972 to revive the 1919 musical comedy *Irene* and make it palatable to new audiences, the hardhats went on and the work began. To overhaul the book, producer Harry Rigby hired two of the best, Joseph Stein (*Fiddler on the Roof*) and Hugh Wheeler (who was also represented that season by his Tony-winning book for *A Little Night Music*), to revise his own adaptation.

The original score, by Harry Tierney and Joseph McCarthy, was considerably altered, with new songs, many by theater vet Wally Harper, inserted alongside the show's classics like "Alice Blue Gown." The presence of Debbie Reynolds, as lovely Irene O'Dare, gave new-fangled star power to the evening, and old pros like George S. Irving and Patsy Kelly made the whole show, despite its many coats of paint, look like a new old-fashioned show, rather than an old vehicle with a tune-up.

Duelling Musicals!
Musicals that Share the Same Source Material

Every so often, a musical will hit the boards with an air of familiarity about it. And often that familiarity is justified: Many musicals share an original source with another show. These twenty musicals examine that kinship.

1. *CYRANO* vs. *CYRANO, THE MUSICAL*

Some would consider a musical version of Rostand's classic play *Cyrano de Bergerac* a waste of time, since the play itself is so beautiful and lyrical. But the period trappings, the romance, and, indeed, the lyricism of the play are surely what draw musical authors to the classic tale of a brilliant yet unattractive man wooing and eventually dying for his vision of perfection.

The 1972 season saw Anthony Burgess adapt his own superb translation into a musical libretto, with music by Michael J. Lewis. The production, an import from Minneapolis's Guthrie Theater, starred Christopher Plummer as Cyrano, and he won raves and a Tony Award, but the production was dismissed as unmemorable. A similar fate befell the version that hit Broadway in 1994 as *Cyrano, the Musical*. This version was a big success in the Netherlands, and the producers decided to chance it on Broadway in a weak season that saw only two successful new musical entries (*Disney's Beauty and the Beast* and *Passion*).

The great wordsmith Sheldon Harnick was asked to polish the lyrics, which were not exactly Broadway-worthy (one example: Cyrano refers to his nose as "a snorer or borer or odor-explorer." *Achoo*!) Despite an energetic performance from Bill van Dijk as The Nose, *Cyrano, the Musical* went the way of *Cyrano* the musical, and faded fast.

2. *KISMET* vs. *TIMBUKTU!*

Two musicals based on the Arabian Nights have made it to Broadway, and they're actually the same show, or almost. *Kismet* (1953), first out of the box, was a color-ful, stylish telling of the Arabian tales based on the play *Kismet* by Edward Knoblock, set to the music of Boro-din's "Polovetsian Dances," adapted by Luther Davis, Robert Wright, and George Forrest. Starring Alfred Drake as the poet Hajj, it was a smash hit.

Davis collaborated with Charles Lederer on the 1978 "African" version, *Timbuktu!* Set in the Mali capi-tal instead of Baghdad for this version, director Geof-frey Holder, following his similarly Afro-centric *The Wiz,* punched up the tribal-ritual trappings inherent in the new setting and gave the role of Saheem-La-Lume, the evil Wazir's bored, sexy wife (known simply as La-lume in *Kismet*) to Eartha Kitt, who entered borne aloft on brawny shoulders, and pretty much didn't come down all night. Both *Kismet* and *Timbuktu!* remained true to the themes of love, life, and death as played against the shifting sands of time.

3.   *THE WILD PARTY* vs. *THE WILD PARTY*

Joseph Moncure March's epic poem *The Wild Party*, about the Jazz Age revels of a fading vaudeville couple, got two, count 'em, two different productions in New York in 2000, both featuring scores by up-and-coming New York composers.

Off-Broadway saw Manhattan Theater Club's production of *The Wild Party*, with a book and score by Andrew Lippa, who had two new songs featured in the Broadway revival *of You're a Good Man, Charlie Brown* the season before. *The Wild Party*, version 2.0, was developed at New York's Public Theater and had a score by Michael John La Chiusa and book by La Chiusa and director George C. Wolfe.

Following much media tongue-wagging focusing on the unusual happenstance surrounding the two shows' proximity, the Lippa version played its subscription run and hoped to transfer to Broadway, but didn't. The Public Theater version did move uptown but won none of its seven Tony nominations, and shuttered soon after the awards ceremony. Both versions of *The Wild Party* got points for trying, but neither was quite able to do justice to the decadence and desperation of the March poem.

4.   *THE GOLDEN APPLE* vs. *HOME SWEET HOMER*

Perhaps nothing short of the Bible (or the Koran) is less suited for Broadway musical adaptation than Homer's *Iliad* and *Odyssey*, at least when played straight, and that's the reason for the wildly different shows that share the source material here.

Home Sweet Homer concerns itself with Homer's quest to return to his wife Penelope, and as a vehicle for the always-intense Yul Brynner, the piece tended to take itself rather too seriously for its own good. Following a legendarily tempestuous and difficult tryout period, *Home Sweet Homer*, totally humorless and charmless, opened and closed on a single day in January 1976.

1954's *The Golden Apple*, on the other hand, is one of the most underappreciated musicals Broadway has ever seen. Composer Jerome Moross and librettist-lyricist John Latouche fashioned a brilliant musical (or, rather, to co-opt a title of a previous Moross-Latouche collaboration, a "Ballet Ballad") from the two Homer epics—first act, *Iliad*, second act, *Odyssey*—but pointed up the theatricality of their enterprise by re-setting the legend in turn-of-the-century Washington state, with its Mount Olympus and golden apples, at the time of the Spanish–American War.

Ulysses and the heroes, agrarians all, are back from Manila and Cuba, unsure of the new industrial century challenging them in the form of the city of Rhododendron, down in the valley. Paris, the very symbol of industry and urban chicanery, is a traveling salesman who dances Helen away in his balloon. Ulysses wins Helen back in a bare-knuckle boxing match before Mayor Hector, the citizenry, and the sirens pick the heroes off little by little, leaving Ulysses alone to re-examine the new century, his wife, and their marriage.

That these weighty ideas play with the speed and breeze of a cyclone is a testament to the authors, who used early-twentieth century musical forms and rhymes (and no dialogue—take *that*, Mr. Brynner) to remove any pretense. About the only thing *Home*

Sweet Homer and *The Golden Apple* have in common, other than the source material, is that *The Golden Apple* was a commercial flop as well.

5. *GODSPELL* vs. *COTTON PATCH GOSPEL*

The Gospel According to St. Matthew is undeniably great drama, and by the evidence offered in these two shows, not bad musical theater either. Stephen Schwartz and John-Michael Tebelak had previously musicalized the story of Christ's last days (Schwartz writing tunes) for Tebelak's master's thesis, and in the anything-goes off-Broadway scene of the early '70s, they put it up with great success. The 1971 production was irreverent and groovy (Jesus was a benevolent clown with a Superman 'S' on his shirt, his disciples lovable ragamuffins) but never blasphemous or overtly preachy.

Harry Chapin's *Cotton Patch Gospel*, from 1981, used the same Gospel (by way of Dr. Clarence Jordan's *Cotton Patch Version of Matthew and John*) to tell Christ's story as a revival-tent show in Gainesville, Georgia. Tom Key and Russel Treyz's book created more obvious modern parallels to the ancient story than *Godspell* (Herod bombs a church nursery to try and kill Jesus; Christ is eventually lynched by Governor Pilate's henchmen), and the mood and the music were contemporary country, with several superb, moving Chapin songs, most notably "Jubilation" and "When I Look Up."

But *Cotton Patch Gospel,* like *Godspell,* offers a vivid witness to the Greatest Story Ever Told, and it's no mystery as to why both are popular in regional and community theaters across the country.

6. *THE BOYS FROM SYRACUSE* vs. *OH, BROTHER!*

Richard Rodgers and Lorenz Hart often wrote in tandem with estimable author/director George Abbott, and *The Boys from Syracuse*, their 1938 effort, may be the best collaboration of them all. The source for *Syracuse* was Shakespeare's *The Comedy of Errors*, which became a snazzy, jazzy farce ("If it's good enough for Shakespeare," the show begins, "it's good enough for us") concerning two sets of mismatched twins and their escapades on one crazy day in Ephesus. A truly great score (featuring the standards "This Can't Be Love" and "Falling in Love With Love," as well as the close-harmony wowza "Sing For Your Supper") led critics to opine that Shakespeare had merely been missing the punch of a Rodgers and Hart score to make his show really work. An unsuccessfully re-written revival hit-Broadway in 2002.

The Comedy of Errors is itself based on Plautus' *The Twin Menachmae*, and in 1981 another musical based on *The Twin Menachmae* hit the Main Stem. The unhappily-titled *Oh, Brother!* reset the twins plot in the contemporary Persian Gulf (yep, a lot of opportunity for Broadway-style musical comedy there). Whatever charm was present in *Syracuse* (not to mention the killer score) didn't translate, and despite a George Abbott-like surfeit of young talent (David-James Carroll, Harry Groener, Mary Mastrantonio, *sans* "Elizabeth"), *Oh, Brother!* lasted only one performance.

7. *THE HOUSE OF MARTIN GUERRE* vs. *THE RETURN OF MARTIN GUERRE*

The tale of Martin Guerre is a true story of a Frenchman who marries, then leaves his home in the Pyrenees village of Artegat to join the army, where he is presumed dead. Years later, a man returns to Artegat, claiming to be Martin Guerre. He is welcomed back, but is later suspected (and finally revealed) to be an impostor. Two musicals based on the true story of Martin Guerre have received high-profile musical stagings—and it seems in the case of this tale, smaller is better.

The House of Martin Guerre opened in Toronto in 1993. The work of two women, Leslie Arden and Anna Theresa Cascio, *House* focused on Martin's long-suffering wife, Bertrande, and the effect of her child-marriage to the loveless Guerre, her eventual attraction to Guerre's impostor, and the eventual awakening of the village to the new world outside their closed doors. A superb production at Chicago's Goodman Theater in 1995, starring Tony-winner Antony Crivello as the impostor, and the wonderful Julain Molnar as Bertrande, gave full voice to this version of the legend as seen from a woman's point of view.

At nearly the same time as *House* was on the boards in Chicago, Cameron Mackintosh's production of *The Return of Martin Guerre* opened in London. Written by Claude-Michel Schönberg and Alain Boublil, who were responsible for Mackintosh's *Les Misérables* and *Miss Saigon*, *The Return of Martin Guerre* had neither the epic sweep of *Les Misérables* nor the tragic stature of *Miss Saigon*, yet was produced with size and bombast similar to those twin behemoths. The show relied on weary storytelling devices as well, originally telling the tale through the narration of a town cripple and a trio of old village biddies who provided heavy-handed comic relief.

8. *BAKER STREET* vs. *SHERLOCK HOLMES*

Sir Arthur Conan Doyle's novels featuring his fictional detective, Sherlock Holmes, are easily the most popular detective novels ever published, and their London locations, colorful villains, and elaborate plots would make them ideal candidates for musicalization. Two top-flight musicals have explored the world of the great gumshoe.

Baker Street, from 1965, was a Big Broadway Musical from the get-go. Directed by Harold Prince, *Baker Street* set its tale at the time of Queen Victoria's Jubilee, pitting Holmes and Dr. Watson against their old nemesis, Professor Moriarty, who wants to pinch the Crown Jewels and get rid of Holmes once and for all. Holmes enlists his Baker Street Irregulars to pursue Moriarty through the alleys and sewers of London. With a then-unheard-of top ticket price of $9.90, *Baker Street* offered stunning, Tony-winning sets by Oliver Smith and a Jubilee parade in the fog by the Bil Baird Marionettes, but the score and script ultimately did the show in. *Baker Street*'s record-breaking grosses dried up quickly, and the show closed in less than a year.

Sherlock Holmes, the Musical, wasn't even that lucky (or even that good, if you ask most people). Veteran tunesmith Leslie Bricusse supplied book, music, and lyrics, with British character man Ron Moody stepping into Holmes' tweed cape and deerstalker hat. Opening in London in 1989, it incorporated much from other Bricusse shows, most notably the opening number, "London is London," which was cribbed from Bricusse's musical *Goodbye, Mr. Chips*. A critical and financial flop, *Holmes* brought to mind the music-hall shows of the previous era, which had been completely eclipsed by the pop-opera spectacles of the '70s and '80s. Moody's presence in *Sherlock Holmes* also invited inevitable comparison to his triumph as Fagin in the infinitely superior *Oliver!* two decades before.

9. *THE PHANTOM OF THE OPERA* vs. *PHANTOM*

Gaston Leroux's celebrated novel of a deformed lunatic living in the bowels of the Paris Opera House had been memorably filmed many times and in many styles, but still it came as no surprise to theater folk when Andrew Lloyd Webber announced his intention to write the music for a stage version. What followed has become perhaps the greatest commercial phenomenon in musical theater history, rivaled only by *Les Miserables* and that other Webber behemoth, *Cats.*

Breathtakingly designed by Maria Bjornson and Andrew Bridge, and directed in high style by Harold Prince, *The Phantom of the Opera* opened in London in 1985 with Webber's wife, Sarah Brightman, as the heroine, ingenue Christine Daae, and Michael Crawford in a mesmerizing turn as the tortured Phantom. A worldwide smash hit, the show had roughly eight thousand touring companies on the road, and a merchandising operation that would make Michael Jordan blush.

Phantom is the simpler title of another musical version from 1991, this one written by the gifted Maury Yeston and Arthur Kopit, who collaborated on the Broadway musical *Nine* in 1982, besting Webber's *Joseph and the Amazing Technicolor Dreamcoat* in the Tony race that year. The Yeston-Kopit *Phantom* has never played Broadway for obvious reasons, but has a rich life in regional and foreign productions (often being billed as the most successful musical never to have played New York). Supporters of the Yeston-Kopit *Phantom* maintain that the storytelling is superior in their version, offering a more compelling relationship between Christine and her father, and portraying the Phantom as a more pathetic, and less mesmerizing, creature of need.

10. *MY DARLIN' AIDA* vs. *AIDA: THE MUSICAL*

Another great idea for a musical: A golden boy, loved by all, son of a conquering war hero, falls in love with a slave, their forbidden romance setting in motion a tragic chain of events. Great, except that Giuseppe Verdi got there first. He turned it into the grand opera *Aida*, which is standard repertory all over the world. Two musicals based on Verdi's work have opened on Broadway, with varying results.

Charles Friedman had directed Oscar Hammerstein's *Carmen Jones*, which Hammerstein had adapted from Bizet's opera *Carmen*, resetting the opera in the black American South. Friedman, not exactly on Hammerstein's level as a writer, adapted Verdi's opera into the Southern gothic *My Darlin' Aida* in 1952. Retaining Verdi's music, Friedman turned ancient Memphis into Memphis, Tennessee, at the time of the Civil War, and changed the characters accordingly (Radames = Ray Demarest, Pharaoh = General Farrow, etc.). The beautifully mounted production came across to most critics like a novelty, music critics mostly saying, "great music," and drama critics saying, "great sets." *My Darlin' Aida* closed after only eighty-nine performances.

Disney Theatricals' Y2K spectacle *Aida*, on the other hand, is still going strong after three-plus years. A blazingly abstract take on the story, *Aida* has a Tony-winning score by Tim Rice and Elton John and book by director Robert Falls, David Henry Hwang and Linda Woolverton. The conceit of this *Aida* has contemporary characters meeting in the Egyptian wing of a museum, ineluctably drawn together as Aida and Radames were long ago, the story subsuming them.

With Elton John supplying good, catchy pop tunes, as is his wont, and Rice doing his usual bit with uninspired lyrics, *Aida* works best as a showcase: visually, by way of Bob Crowley's stunning, abstract-modern sets and costumes, and musically, with killer pop roles in Aida, Radames, and spoiled little rich girl Amneris.

The Wages of Sin
TV Shows Featuring Broadway Stars

B roadway has long been the proving ground for television and movie success. If you don't think so, look up the calendar year that actress Mercedes Ruehl had between May of 1991 and April of 1992. Following are ten television shows featuring performers from Broadway's musical stages.

1. *OZ*

HBO's just-ended unflinching prison drama featured three fine musical performers in vastly different roles: J.K. Simmons (*Guys and Dolls*) as pitiless neo-Nazi Schillinger, B.D. Wong as Father Ray, and Rita Moreno as Sister Peter Marie. (Wong played Linus in the revival of *You're a Good Man, Charlie Brown*; Moreno was in the one-performance disaster *Gantry*.) Both Wong and Moreno are Tony winners for plays, and Moreno, of course, won an Oscar for her superb performance as Anita in *West Side Story*.

2. *WILL AND GRACE*

The chic sitcom about ultra-hip New Yorkers is riddled with ultra-professional Broadway talent. Emmy winners Eric McCormack (who played in *Meredith Will-son's The Music Man* in 2001), as good-guy Will Truman, and Megan Mullally (Rizzo in *Grease*, Rose-mary in 1995's *How to Succeed . . .* revival), who plays quippy socialite Karen Walker, trade the witty, bitchy repartee that is their show's trademark. The late Greg-ory Hines, whose Broadway musical career spanned almost 40 years, used to pop up occasionally as Will's boss, Ben Doucette. He's been replaced by Willy Wonka himself (or is it Leo Bloom?), Gene Wilder, who recently won an Emmy for his portrayal of mercurial Mr. Stein.

3.   *ONE OF THE BOYS*

One of the who? Nineteen eighty-what, now? This for-gettable NBC sitcom from 1982 is worth mentioning only for its cast: Amidst the predictable sitcom detritus were future stars Dana Carvey and Meg Ryan, joined by a manic character guy named Nathan Lane. Lane is Broadway royalty now, with two Tonys and tons of fans and goodwill.

The old guard was represented by veterans Scat-man Crothers and Mr. Mickey Rooney. Rooney made a belated Broadway debut in 1979's burlesque riot *Sugar Babies*. His last Main Stem appearance to date was in the waning days of *The Will Rogers Follies*, as Will's father, Clem.

4.   *THE WEST WING*

Fictional First Lady Abigail Bartlet is played by the magnificent Stockard Channing, who made her Broad-way debut in 1971's *Two Gentlemen of Verona* and was also in *They're Playing Our Song* and took over for Liza Minnelli in *The Rink*. On the *West Wing* set she can swap backstage stories with Dulé Hill, who plays Charlie Young, the personal aide to the President. Hill scored on Broadway in 1996's *Bring in 'da Noise Bring in 'da Funk*. *The West Wing* seems to be gathering Tony winners like kudzu; recently joining the cast were the fabulous Joanna Gleason (*Into the Woods*), as counsel Jordan Kendall, Mary-Louise Parker (2001's Best Play *Proof*), as Amy Gardner, and Lily Tomlin (1986's *The Search for Signs of Intelligent Life in the Universe*) playing the President's secretary, Debbie Fiderer.

5. *LAW & ORDER*

The song-and-dancing-est cops on TV are Ed Green and Lenny Briscoe, or, as they're better known, Jesse L. Martin and Jerry Orbach. *Law & Order*'s detectives both boast Broadway musical credits, Martin making a splash as the first Tom Collins in the mega-hit *Rent*. Orbach has a list of credits as long as your arm, among them creating the role of El Gallo off-Broadway in *The Fantasticks*, singing the role of Lumiere in Disney's great film version of *Beauty and the Beast*, and creating roles in *Carnival* and Bob Fosse's original production of *Chicago*. Their TV boss, S. Epatha Merkerson, scored a huge triumph as Billie Holliday in *Lady Day at Emerson's Bar & Grill* off-Broadway in 1987.

6. *LATE SHOW WITH DAVID LETTERMAN*

Broadcasting from the heart of the theater district at 1697 Broadway, *Late Show With David Letterman* often hosts big-time Broadway stars to go along with Dave's Big-Ass Ham. And look, behind the keyboards! It's Paul Shaffer! Letterman's longtime musical director got his start in Canada, and, following a legendary production of Stephen Schwartz's *Godspell* in Toronto,

Shaffer took the job of Musical Director for *Godspell*'s move from off-Broadway to Broadway in 1976. Shaffer also served as Musical Director for Gilda Radner's live evening on Broadway in 1979.

7. *THE DICK Van DYKE SHOW*

TV's greatest sitcom was set in the New York suburb of New Rochelle, its star working as head writer for a Sid Caesar-style variety show in the city. It stood to reason that much of the show's classic humor would be Broadway-related. After debuting on Broadway in *The Girls Against the Boys*, Dick Van Dyke gave a memorable performance as Albert Peterson in *Bye Bye Birdie*; he also headlined the 1981 revival of *The Music Man*.

His TV costars, Rose Marie (*Top Banana*) and the versatile Morey Amsterdam, who wrote two original Broadway revues, added much-needed authenticity. Mary Tyler Moore, as hottest-housewife-ever Laura Petrie, never appeared on Broadway in a musical, but was Holly Golightly in the legendary road disaster *Breakfast at Tiffany's*.

8. *SEX and THE CITY*

Sarah Jessica Parker, the star of HBO's *Sex and the City*, has appeared on Broadway four times, three of them in musicals (working her way up the orphanage to star in *Annie*, as the star of the 1997 revival of *Once Upon a Mattress*, and opposite her soon-to-be husband Matthew Broderick in *How to Succeed inBusiness Without Really Trying*). *Sex and the City* lives and breathes its New York locations, and as such, the cream of the Broadway crop is often featured, such as Nathan Lane as a society pianist, or Mary Testa as a cabaret siren.

9. *THE SOPRANOS*

Jamie-Lynn DiScala plays Meadow Soprano, troubled daughter to a mobster, on HBO's great drama series *The Sopranos*. DiScala, who has also released a pop album, made her Broadway debut as Belle in *Disney's Beauty and the Beast* in the fall of 2002. Her *Sopranos* grandfather, Tom Aldredge, is a two-time Tony nominee and a favorite of Stephen Sondheim and James Lapine, who have used him in *Into the Woods* and *Passion*. *Sopranos* Production Designer Bob Shaw is a favorite designer at the Public Theater as well.

10. *ALL MY CHILDREN*

With a few exceptions, all daytime soap operas are taped in New York, so many actors do soaps all day, then head to the theater at night. Actor James Mitchell, who plays Palmer Cortland on *All My Children*, is a Broadway hoofer from way back, appearing in the original cast of the classic *Brigadoon* as sword-dancing Harry Beaton. He was also seen in shows as diverse as *Mack and Mabel* and *Carnival*, as well as in a memorable role in the great movie tuner *The Band Wagon*. And, of course, the glamorous Susan Lucci, a/k/a Erica Kane, de-glammed for a stint in *Annie Get Your Gun* back in 2000.

Fill the World with Ships and Shoes

10 Musicals about Big Business

There is a category of Broadway show known as the "tired businessman show." These shows feature corny plots, big sets and costumes, and girls, girls, girls, all designed to soothe the gray-flannel type who has collapsed into his seat. Here are ten musicals that hit close to home for Joe Bottomline.

1. *HOW TO SUCCEED IN BUSINESS WITHOUT REALLY TRYING*

Maybe the funniest musical in Broadway history, *How to Succeed . . .* won the Pulitzer Prize for1961–62, and multiple Tonys as well. Adapted from Shepherd Mead's satirical novel of the same name, it concerns a ruthless young climber of the corporate ladder and the many rungs he encounters on his way.

What makes the show so funny and so successful is that there really are no heroes. Every single character is pretty horrid (or boldly ambitious, at least) in his or her own right, and book writer Abe Burrows and com-

Greg Kolack/Drury Lane theater, Oak Brook, Illinois

In this scene from *How to Succeed in Business without Really Trying,* perhaps the funniest musical ever written, the protagonist, Finch, makes his pitch to the board of World Wide Wickets. This photo is from a production at the Drury Lane Theater in suburban Chicago. The author is sitting at the table, fifth from the left.

poser-lyricist Frank Loesser never let heart or sentiment get in the way of the laughs or the show as a whole.

2. *URINETOWN*

A riotous spoof of big business and the conventions of the stage musical, *Urinetown* was 2001's "Little musical that could," moving from off-off Broadway to the big time and three Tony awards.

Urinetown concerns UCG, Urine Good Company, a pay-toilet monopoly in a metropolis with a water shortage. UGC tells everyone, Huxley-like, that it's a "Privilege to Pee," and the no-good big boss Caldwell B. Cladwell keeps a tight fist on the big bucks. Sparks fly as the good folk of the village rebel against the System, and all is done with an eye winking madly at the audience (the security guards at UGC are Officers Lockstock and Barrel, the heroine is named Little Sally, etc.) and lines in the script directly addressing the question of why musicals are written the way they are. Due to its great success, *Urinetown* may well be the future of the musical theater as we know it: small, relatively cheap, and deconstructionist.

3. *HOW NOW, DOW JONES*

Generally regarded as a mediocre show with perhaps the stupidest plot of the postwar era, *How Now, Dow Jones* at least has a catchy title and the semi-standard march tune "Step to the Rear." But oh, that plot!

If you can stand it, read on: Kate, who announces the Dow Jones numbers, has a boyfriend who won't marry her until the Dow Jones hits 1000. (Oh, dear.) She gets pregnant by another guy and arbitrarily announces the DJIA has hit 1000. (Oh, my.) After the market collapses, the oldest man on Wall Street buys everything, and all and sundry are paired off in the end. (Oh, forget it.)

Lyricist Carolyn Leigh was to blame for the idea, and "Abominable Showman" David Merrick was to blame for bringing the show in to Broadway in 1967. Shame, shame, stupid shame.

4. *FLAHOOLEY*

A wild satire of politics, capitalism, and fanaticism, *Flahooley* was about a toymaker who develops a new doll, the Flahooley, that saturates and then collapses the market. That's a thumbnail outline, because *Flahooley* had plot enough for five shows.

The market floods because Flahooleys are being made by a genie who doesn't want to return to his lamp; the lamp has been brought to "Toycoon" B.G. Bigelow by an Arabian consortium intent on solving their oil crisis; Flahooleys are burned in public and the genie is hunted down with McCarthy-like zeal; the puppets from the toy factory *sing* the opening number. A truly fine score by Sammy Fain and E.Y. Harburg offset the wacky book by Harburg and Fred Saidy, which many saw as too critical of the American way and un-comfortably non-conformist, especially in the wake of World War II.

5. *THE ROTHSCHILDS*

The great songwriting team of Jerry Bock and Sheldon Harnick (*Fiddler on the Roof, Fiorello!*) wrote this 1971 musical, along with librettist Sherman Yellen. Hal Linden played Mayer Rothschild, the head of the legend-ary European moneylending family.

As musical biographies go, it was solid, if unre-markable, save for the use of European anti-Semitism as a plot device. Attacks on the family's property con-tinue unabated through their lives, and, despite their success, they are also taunted, often by children, as second-class citizens. The musical ends at court, with Europe's crowned heads finally recognizing the fami-ly's greatness, bowing to Rothschild's sons as they are made baronets.

6. *THE BEST LITTLE WHOREHOUSE GOES PUBLIC*

A sequel to the 1977 hit *The Best Little Whorehouse in Texas*, which told the semi-true story of the Chicken

Ranch, an illegal but cherished Texas institution, 1994's *The Best Little Whorehouse Goes Public* took the idea of a legal brothel and applied some mid-90's business savvy to it.

Madam Mona Stangley, the heroine of the first show, is asked to run another brothel by an old flame, and soon she decides to float the place on the stock exchange. The IRS gets wind of it, and chaos ensues. Called to Washington to testify, Mona charms Congress, the press, and the American people, who soon elect her President. Rrrright.

Public was a sixteen-performance flop, mainly because the "titillation factor" inherent in seeing a show with a dirty title back in the '70s has all but vanished. The Vegas-tacky sense of grunge permeating the whole enterprise didn't help, either.

7. FINIAN'S RAINBOW

Another Yip Harbug-Fred Saidy triumph, *Finian's Rainbow* (with music by Burton Lane) is scattershot satire with a perfect score. Mainly a political satire, there are still many swipes at big business and the postwar boom.

Irishman Finian McLonergan has stolen a crock of gold from a leprechaun and has traveled stateside to place it next to Fort Knox, where, like all US dollars, it will grow. Finian unites with sharecroppers to foil a crooked Senator and reclaim Rainbow Valley. The sharecroppers cheerfully harvest tobacco because it's all they know how to do. When they get wind of the gold, they call up the great chain store of Shears, Robust and have an orgy of buying, represented by the rousing numbers "The Great Come-and-get-it Day" and "When the Idle Poor Become the Idle Rich."

8. *THE PaJaMa GaME*

The age-old battle of labor vs. management is the issue in *The Pajama Game*, a thoroughly charming 1954 musical about union problems at the Sleep Rite Pajama Factory in Cedar Rapids, Iowa. (Full disclosure: The author attended college in Cedar Rapids, and no such factory exists, and if it does, the employees certainly don't sing and dance there.)

Since it's a musical, *The Pajama Game's* leads (he's management, she's labor) must fall in love, but more interesting is what goes on around them. Pre-dating *How to Succeed . . .* 's musicalized coffee break and rooftop party, *The Pajama Game* sets to music a company picnic (the joyous "Once-a-year Day") and even a union meeting (the insanely cued but sizzling "Steam Heat").

q. *PROMISES, PROMISES*

Love and sex masquerade as business and power in this 1968 musical version of the classic 1960 film *The Apartment*. Jerry Orbach played a likable corporate Everyman whose bosses often used his nifty apartment for their trysts. The schlub then falls for his boss's latest conquest, played by the appealing Jill O'Hara.

A state-of-the-art show, *Promises* was the last of a dying breed. Its success made it one of the final old-fashioned musical comedies to work on Broadway. Neil Simon wrote the ingratiating book, and Burt Bacharach and Hal David's score explored pop sounds relatively unfamiliar to Broadway at the time. Their use of a vocal group in the pit pre-dated the "Vocal Minority" pit voices in *Company*.

10. *PACIFIC OVERTURES*

The Westernization (and, ultimately, industrialization) of Japan by the United States was examined in this powerful 1976 Stephen Sondheim-Harold Prince musical. Prince directed the show, with a book by John Weidman, in Kabuki style, using only actors of Asian descent, to examine Commodore Perry's voyage to Japan from the Japanese point of view.

One striking book scene examined American missionary/businessman Jonathan Goble, who invented the rickshaw ("Powered by Japanese"), and the finale of the musical, "Next," threw Japan from the agrarian mid-nineteenth century into the highly industrialized post-war twentieth century. An uncompromising but ravishingly beautiful show in both look and sound, *Pacific Overtures* was a Bicentennial poison-pen letter to both big business and politics.

That Was a Flop?

10 Misleadingly Great
Broadway Cast Albums

As a direct marketing tool, the Original Cast Album ranks up there with the "George Foreman Grill" and the "ThighMaster." Cast albums are so persuasive that they can often disguise a flop as a brilliant-sounding hit. Thanks to their original recordings, here are nine shows that sounded better than they actually were, and one show that actually worked in reverse: wringing a terrible cast album from a masterpiece.

1. *CANDIDE*

The granddaddy of all flop cast albums. The Leonard Bernstein-Richard Wilbur score (with additional lyrics by John LaTouche and Dorothy Parker, plus Bernstein himself) is one of the musical theater's very, very best, working wonderfully as operetta, operetta parody, even twelve-tone serialism.

Unfortunately, the score, as preserved on the price-less 1956 original cast album, obscures the fact that the show was indeed a failure, Lillian Hellman's McCarthy-allegory libretto registering as too heavy-handed and untrue to Voltaire's picaresque tale of Candide and his one-joke optimism. Tyrone Guthrie's drag-queens-at-the-prom staging didn't help, either. Better to revel in the performances of Barbara Cook, Robert Rounseville, and William Olvis.

(Note: *Candide* re-entered the Broadway consciousness in 1974, thanks to that original cast album. Harold Prince's environmental staging at off-Broadway's Chelsea Theater Certer was brought downtown and installed at the reconfigured Broadway Theater. The cast album of *that* production, Hugh Wheeler's new dialogue included, does the show a mild disservice, reducing the orchestra almost to combo size, and emphasizing the production's madcap, thrift-store atmosphere.)

2. *GREENWILLOW*

Frank Loesser wrote this musical adaptation of B.J. Chute's novel, a fantasy of a twee little village where cows act as currency, folks bake bilberry tarts, and two ministers (Mutt and Jeff, basically) preach the Word at opposite ends of the spectrum. "Loesser goes bucolic" is how many describe the score. "Really good" is another way of putting it, as this Son of Tin Pan Alley adapted well to the folkish atmosphere of Chute's novel. "The Music of Home," "Clang-Dang the Bell," "Could've Been a Ring"—these are not titles one would exactly mistake for numbers out of *Guys and Dolls*.

The cast album, led by Anthony Perkins (really!) and the marvelous Pert Kelton, makes the show seem better than it really is. The book, written by Loesser and Lesser Samuels, meanders as much as Greenwillow's Meander River, and it runs out of steam in the second act (the aforementioned cow is the centerpiece of much of the drama). *Greenwillow* is an uneven show, but the cast album shows us that the score captured the hoped-for mood much better than the book, design, or direction did.

3. *TINTYPES*

Another small-scale musical out of place on Broadway (it transferred from off-Broadway's ANTA Theater), *Tintypes* is a revue-style trip through the popular music of the Gay Nineties up to the dawn of World War I. Conceived by pianist-musical director Mel Marvin for a small band and a cast of five, the show lasted through the Christmas holiday in 1980, but closed in January of 1981.

The good news is that Tony nominations (though no awards) followed, and a cast album was released. The original cast recording of *Tintypes* is a double-album (remember those?) feast of over forty songs by over twenty-five songwriters, including Victor Herbert, Scott Joplin, and John Philip Sousa, and winningly performed by the excellent original cast, which featured future Tony winners Jerry Zaks and the late Lynne Thigpen. To add to the good fortune, the fledgling Arts and Entertainment cable network filmed a studio production using the cast album tracks, preserving the whole show, ensuring its future as a regional and community-theater staple for years to come.

Mary Kyte's musical staging and Gary Pearle's direction attractively concealed a slight overall concept (distinct song and sketch sets depicting industrial progress, immigration, vaudeville, etc.), but the collection of songs, as performed by the cast who put them over from the very beginning, were what made *Tintypes* so special.

4. *MERRILY WE ROLL ALONG*

Stephen Sondheim is contemporary Broadway's dominant composer-lyricist, and as such, every move he makes demands attention. All eyes were on Sondheim, librettist George Furth, and director Harold Prince as they opened their new musical, *Merrily We Roll Along*, in New York, without the benefit of an out-of-town fix-it period. *Merrily*'s 1981 preview period is legendary, marked by cast changes, a fired choreographer, an almost complete costume overhaul, and some of the worst buzz ever accorded a musical in New York previews. The writing was on the wall when *Merrily* finally opened, and the show had only a two-week run.

Almost all the critics were unanimous in their reviews: Furth's unappealing, quippy-kooky book was a shambles and not well served by Prince's decision to cast the show entirely with unpolished teenagers. Also muddy was the entire motive for the show: a backwards-in-time examination of the vagaries of success and friendship as visited upon three longtime friends and colleagues.

What did work, as all acknowledged, was Sondheim's score, and it remains the most exuberant, fresh, and, yes, *youthful* score he's written since his first, the seldom-seen *Saturday Night*. But while it seems unthinkable that a Sondheim show would go unrecorded, *Merrily*, due to its failure, was never a lead-pipe cinch. But record producer Thomas Z. Shepard, showing the characteristic zeal of the show's antihero, Franklin Shepard, gave the score a first-class treatment on disc. (The packaging of the album was outstanding, too.)

It was his stated intention to make the show sound better on record than it ever did in the theater, and the hitherto-raw cast was focused brilliantly in the record-ing studio. The result was a heartbreakingly emotional recording, with "Good Thing Going," the cheer-up rouser "Now You Know," and the brilliantly hopeful "Our Time" particular standouts. Absent the confusing staging concept and George Furth's odd book, the cast album of *Merrily We Roll Along* sounds like it belongs to a smash hit.

5. ***MACK & MABEL***

Jerry Herman's stock dipped a bit after the flop *Dear World*; he waited over five years to return to Broadway. After being approached with the idea of a musical about silent-film king Mack Sennett and his unconven-tional romance with his muse, Mabel Normand, he took his time working on it. *Mack and Mabel* opened on Broadway in early October of 1974, but only lasted for 66 performances, closing at the end of November. The show's creative team (producer David Merrick, direc-tor-choreographer Gower Champion, librettist Michael Stewart, and Herman) had created a monster hit with *Hello, Dolly!*, but, despite two glowing stars (Robert Preston and Bernadette Peters) and eight Tony nomi-nations, they couldn't duplicate the feat with *M & M*.

The problematic book came in for most of the criti-cism: Mack Sennett's lack of warmth ("I won't send roses," he tells Mabel over and over) is not endearing, and the overall arc for both characters is bleak. Sennett is made obscure with the advent of talkies, and Mabel Normand died before her time, enmeshed in drugs and scandal. Add to all that the difficulty of capturing the legendary comedy of the Keystone Kops onstage, and *Mack and Mabel* was hamstrung from the start.

But Herman, who had taken the time to get it right

on his end, provided a strong score (controversially, not Tony-nominated) in his usual vein: Clickety-clack character numbers and superb ballads. The cast album leaves the listener, again, wondering how a flop can contain such gems as Bernadette Peters' 'Hey, Ma' number, "Look What Happened to Mabel," or what is perhaps the strongest ballad Herman has ever written, "Time Heals Everything."

6. *HOUSE OF FLOWERS*

It's hard to pin down the reasons why this 1954 show didn't succeed. To listen to the score is to marvel at the good fortune that great writers have in creating songs for dramatic characters; this score positively vibrates with sensuality.

The work of composer Harold Arlen and librettist-lyricist Truman Capote (who got the idea for the tale whilst vacationing in Haiti), *House of Flowers* told the story of Madam Fleur and her "house of flowers," girls named Pansy, Gladiola, etc., and the arrival of a new "flower" who ignites personal and professional chaos on the island. Pearl Bailey, who nine years earlier had scored with Arlen's songs in her Broadway debut, *St. Louis Woman*, was difficult from the get-go, stealing material from other actors and refusing to cooperate with director Peter Brook after he was fired and rehired.

Then again, Bailey was great onstage, and some feel the very gay point of view of the material was what kept it from succeeding. But oh, that score.

7. *JUNO*

Marc Blitzstein was one of the American theater's most talented and versatile composers; his work ranged from conventional theater works such as *Regina*, his opera based on Hellman's *The Little Foxes*, and his version of the Brecht-Weill *Threepenny Opera*, to *Reuben Reuben*, an avant-garde work about a man who can't communicate, and *Juno*, based on Sean O'Casey's play *Juno and the Paycock*.

Juno was faithful to O' Casey's play, which is pretty much a laundry list of woe and misery from strife-torn Ireland, circa 1924. Blitzstein's score, however, soars above the material; "I Wish It So" and "What Is the Stars?" are superb ballads, and the opening number, "We're Alive," is a perfect, colors-flying rouser.

8. *PACIFIC OVERTURES*

Stephen Sondheim, Harold Prince, and John Weidman's Bicentennial musical is a brilliant examination of America's policies of manifest destiny and global capitalism. Telling its story from the Japanese side, in Kabuki style, however, pretty much assured the show of going the way of all flesh.

There was nothing amiss in Sondheim's score, however. Drawing heavily on the Eastern pentatonic scale and avoiding heavy Western rhyme schemes for its Asian characters, the cast album of *Pacific Overtures* is virtually perfect, brilliantly sung by an all-Asian cast. Particularly effective are the numbers "Poems," and the massive history lesson "Please Hello," which may be the funniest song Sondheim has ever written.

9. *THE GOLDEN APPLE*

This bold and creative resetting of *The Iliad* and *The Odyssey* was hailed upon its off-Broadway premiere in at the Phoenix Theater in 1954 and was greeted with even better notices when it moved uptown. But the audiences never came to see *The Golden Apple*, and it closed after only 125 performances. But the fifties saw the cast album explosion, so something this good was bound to reach vinyl.

But since *The Golden Apple* was a genre-bending folk opera, completely sung with no dialogue, cuts had to be made to preserve the score on LP. Lyricist John LaTouche reportedly whipped up rhyming continuity on the spot to patch over the severe cuts made to Jerome Moross's brilliant music. And brilliant it is: Still heard on the album are the gorgeous "Windflowers," Kaye Ballard's hymn of seduction, "Lazy Afternoon," and much of "The Judgment of Paris," the hilarious county fair bake-off to win Paris's favor.

10. *FOLLIES*

Stephen Sondheim and James Goldman's brilliant 1971 musical was one of the musically richest shows ever heard on Broadway. So what's up with the one-disc hatchet job of the brilliant original cast? Again, the song-and-dance team of Ego and Hubris take the prize.

Follies producer-director Hal Prince was reportedly sore at CBS Studios, who had so brilliantly recorded the previous Sondheim score, *Company*, so he made a rather capricious deal with Capitol Records, which didn't have a whole lot of experience with original cast albums. The resultant recording was, to put it mildly, a piece of crap. Many of the brilliant pastiche songs were trimmed and large sections of music cut altogether to make the show fit on a single, two-sided disc. "Irresponsible" is the word often bandied about when this album is discussed. In 1985, RCA Victor thankfully recorded the all-star gala *Follies in Concert* with the New York Philharmonic.

Cinema Theatricalo
Movies about the Creation of Musical Theater

Theater is easily the most cinematic art form. After movies. And, ok, maybe TV. And records can be kind of cinematic, too, right? Anyway, here are ten movies which deal with the creation of musical theater.

1. *TOPSY-TURVY*

Mike Leigh's masterful examination of the great Gibert and Sullivan, the Victorian era, and the circumstances which led them to create their most popular operetta, *The Mikado*. It's a near miracle that a movie this richly detailed and luxurious, in time as well as content, was made in 1999, even in England.

2. *MEETING VENUS*

Glenn Close is a superb singing actress, but it's doubtful she could sing Wagner. Nevertheless, she plays a temperamental Swedish diva (dubbed by Kiri Te Kanawa) in Istvan Szabo's film *Meeting Venus*, a pseudo-documentary look at an international production of *Tannhaüser*. The personal affairs and petty jealousies of the opera folk are amusing (some have seen the muti-national feel of this 1991 film as a metaphor for German reunification), but the climactic *Tannhaüser* itself is dullsville.

3. *CRADLE WILL ROCK*

Tim Robbins's delightful 1999 look at the creation of Marc Blitzstein's political musical *The Cradle Will Rock*, whose opening (and closing) night became famous as the swan song of the Federal Theater Project. Robbins examines big business, the state of the art, and culture wars with a freewheeling cinematic sensibility and a cast of Hollywood stars (Vanessa Redgrave, Susan Sarandon, John Cusack) and New York theater veterans (Paul Giamatti, Cherry Jones, Barnard Hughes).

4. **42nd STREET**

Pretty Lady must go on—even if the star twists an ankle. And you, Peggy Sawyer, are going to save the day! That's the plot of 1933's great *42nd* Street, the corniest and most wonderful backstage musical ever filmed, based on Bradford Ropes's novel. Lloyd Bacon directed, Busby Berkeley (of course) staged the socko numbers, and Ruby Keeler shone as the girl who went out there a youngster, but who came back a star. Broadway's version, first seen in 1980, is heavily influenced by the film.

5. *THE BAND WAGON*

Another great fictional backstager, molded closely on real life. One of Vincente Minnelli's last great M-G-M musicals, Fred Astaire basically plays himself (star dancer past his prime, looking for one last stage hit),

Oscar Levant and Nanette Fabray are basically writers Betty Comden and Adolph Green, and the tyrannical director is played by Jack Buchanan, basically playing . . . Vincente Minnelli. Don't miss Astaire and Cyd Charisse all-timing it to "Dancing in the Dark."

6. *AMADEUS*

It's really about Antonio Salieri's frustration at Mozart's seemingly divine genius, but Peter Shaffer's screenplay of his stage hit, brilliantly directed by Milos Forman, gives us tantalizing glimpses into Mozart's Herculean *oeuvre*, from the highs of the Royal command premiere of *Abduction from the Seraglio* to the lows of the working-class shenanigans of *The Magic Flute*, all wittily staged by Twyla Tharp.

7. *SHOWGIRLS*

Nomi's not a whore, she's a dancer! Good-yet-violently-unstable girl goes to Vegas, becomes a lapdancer, then a stripper, then the star of the fabulous Las Vegas review "Goddess," in Paul Verhoeven's godawful backstager-for-the-nineties, *Showgirls*. As many people have noted, her career trajectory would probably be reversed, since strippers make more money than showgirls, but hey, a semi-nude job's a semi-nude job. Elizabeth Berkley is our toothy heroine; watch her trip another bitchy showgirl down the stairs, mwahahaha.

8. *ALL THAT JAZZ*

A cinema *a clef* if ever one existed, *All That Jazz*, egomaniac supreme Bob Fosse's rumination on his life and work, breathes Broadway from its very pores. A look at talented workaholic and Renaissance man Joe Gideon's struggles to finish a movie ("The Comedian," based on *Lenny*) and get his new Broadway show *NY/LA* (which gives us the fabulous "Take Off With Us/Air Rotica" sequence) up and running, all while enduring open-heart surgery. *All That Jazz* features many of Fosse's theater colleagues, some (Anne Reinking, Ben Vereen) playing characters based on themselves.

9. *BABES ON BROADWAY*

Mickey Rooney and Judy Garland made approximately 7,000 movies together, all about the same thing: Hey kids, let's put on a show! And then we'll take it to Broadway! These incredibly realistic showbiz tales are exemplified by *Babes on Broadway*, directed by (who else) Busby Berkley. The film is basically an excuse for a series of wacky production numbers, in which Judy and Mickey and the kids put on a show and then take it to Broadway. In a theater the size of a Hollywood sound-stage.

10. *THE PRODUCERS*

Mel Brooks's first movie was the basis for the 2001 hit musical of the same name. Set at the time it was made, 1968 (unlike the stage show), it concerns a second-rate producer (Zero Mostel) who cooks up a scheme to make a killing by producing a flop musical. That flop is, of course, *Springtime for Hitler*. Brilliantly cast and completely unafraid, it's not only one of the most quotable movie comedies ever, but also very canny about the theater, thanks in large part to choreographer Alan Johnson's hilarious *Springtime* staging.

Food, Glorious Food!
10 Broadway Musicals You Could Eat

Hungry? Most Broadway theaters have a snack bar for the intermission munchies, but here are ten musicals to satisfy your appetite for something more (which is also the title of a musical, but not a musical about food).

1. *THE GOLDEN APPLE*

Brilliant, near-operatic resetting of Homer's *Iliad* and *Odyssey* in turn-of-the-century Washington state. In this version, written by John Latouche and Jerome Moross, Helen is a randy (and bored) farmer's daughter married to Sheriff Menelaus, and Paris is a dancing salesman who spirits her away in his balloon. General Ulysses and the heroes, cleverly renamed (Bluey for Philoctetes, Thirsty for Tantalus, and Doc MacCahan for Machaon) are back from the Spanish-American War and are eventually guilt-tripped into laying waste to Rhododendron In order to get Helen back.

2. *RAISIN*

This 1973 musical adaptation of Lorraine Hansberry's classic play *A Raisin In the Sun* is fairly faithful to

Hansberry's powerful study of a family's dreams deferred by outside and inside influences. The Judd Woldin-Robert Brittan score got down and dirty when called for ("Booze," where Walter Lee Younger envisions his new liquor store), but also soared, especially in the superb "Measure the Valleys," a mother's plea for understanding of her son. *Raisin* brightened a lean year for Broadway musicals, and it won the Best Musical Tony in 1974.

3. *SHERRY!*

The late Dolores Gray (as sexpot movie queen Lorraine Sheldon) tried her best to liven up this leaden musical adaptation of *The Man Who Came to Dinner*, with TV's *Inside the Actors Studio* host/suckup James Lipton partially to blame; he wrote the lyrics. Critics and audiences pointed right away to the unnecessary expansion of the great Kaufman-Hart play, here blown up to include scenes of the whole town of Sherwood, Ohio ("Smalltown, U.S.A."—how original), with the zany locals brought on for pointless and needless production numbers. It lasted less than two months in 1967.

4. *SUGAR*

Jule Styne and Bob Merrill adapted the great film comedy *Some Like it Hot* for the stage in 1972. Not directed by Billy Wilder. Not in black-and-white. Not starring Marilyn Monroe. What's the point? Broadway audiences felt likewise, despite the presence of old hands like Robert Morse and Tony Roberts and a drop-dead gorgeous Elaine Joyce as Sugar Kane. But the show (often retitled *Some Like it Hot*, for obvious reasons) continues to thrive in regional theater, whose audiences more readily appreciate the drag comedy and inevitable roaring-twenties hoofing. Tony Curtis toured the show in the role of nerdy Osgood during 2002 and 2003.

5. *MILK AND HONEY*

Jerry "*Hello, Dolly!*" Herman waxes affectionate for Israel in this 1961 musical about new settlers and tourists in the Holy Land. Yiddish theater vet Molly Picon leads a pack of middle-aged Jewish-American widows looking for husbands. Herman's Broadway debut gave a glimpse of the great things to come (although his "Hymn to Hymie" was not a tribute to *My Fair Maidel,* rather a widow's paean to her dead husband). The first Broadway musical actually *set* in Israel, *Milk and Honey* was warm but also realistic about the trouble facing settlers in the territory.

6. *THE COCOANUTS*

Irving Berlin wrote the score, George S. Kaufman wrote the book, and it starred the Marx Brothers. It's about a mayonnaise factory in Idaho. Just kidding. It's Minnie's boys running amok in the resort hotel business, circa late 1925. Not one of Berlin's most stellar scores, the brothers filmed it in 1929, giving them a leg up on the art of screen comedy, which they would soon redefine, despite the staginess of this particular film. (Now you know why the film version of *The Cocoanuts* looks like a filmed stage musical: because it was.)

7. *SUGAR BABIES*

Mickey Rooney as Top Banana and Ann Miller as The Legs in this unabashed, smash-hit tribute to the great days of burlesque, with jugglers, ventriloquists, corny gags (in one sketch, Miller, as Mrs. Westfall, is referred to by the leering Judge Rooney as "Mrs. Breastfall" and "Mrs. Bestball") and pretty chorus gals galore (the Sugar Babies of the title, here swinging like Evelyn Nesbit, and there dancing like Lillian Russell). A hit in 1980, *Sugar Babies* was perhaps the last successful evening of burlesque that Broadway will ever see.

8. *THE ROTHSCHILDS*

Hal Linden won a Tony for his portrayal of Mayer Rothschild, paterfamilias of the legendary European moneylenders. This show did not shy away from the anti-Semitism endured by Rothschild and his sons, but rather used the many attacks on their property and persons ("Jew, do your duty!" they were often told, meaning they were expected to bow and scrape in public) as dramatic motivation for their triumphs. The book, by Sherman Yellen, and the score, by the estimable Jerry Bock and Sheldon Harnick, played mainly to the Jewish theater-party crowds and saw *The Rothschilds* to a middling 505-performance run.

9. *THE THREE MUSKETEERS*

Rudolf Friml's 1928 operetta version of the Dumas classic, which somebody thought was just right for revival on the Broadway scene in 1984. Nope. A new libretto by the estimable Mark Bramble held forth the promise of a modern take on the Friml-Wodehouse-Grey warhorse. Unfortunately, nothing could offset the basic fustiness of the genre and the costume-drama trappings. Instead of settling in for a Marathon run and a nice Payday, this Dum Dum's version of *The Three Musketeers* drew nothing but Snickers and became a nine-performance Milk Dud.

10.   *Top Banana*

The legendary Phil Silvers gave a blazing performance in this 1950 show about a burlesque clown (named Jerry Biffle, but bearing a resemblance to a certain TV funnyman whose name rhymes with "Hilton Girl") and his increasingly obsolete TV show, ladling the schtick on top of the corn like melted butter. The score was by Johnny Mercer, but there was no "Moon River" or "Ac-Cent-Chu-Ate the Positive" in this one; the show was really a flimsy excuse for Silvers and some other assured comic hands to cut up, early and often.

Cold and Dead
10 Musicals about Killers

The most heinous crimes often demand the most serious examination of our values. So it's no mystery why killers might occupy the minds of many musical authors.

1. ***SWEENEY TODD, THE DEMON BARBER OF FLEET STREET***

This 1979 musical is near the top of many musical "Best" lists. Stephen Sondheim and Hugh Wheeler's "musical thriller" is based on the English legend of Sweeney Todd, a crazy barber who slit the throats of his customers while they were in his chair, and gave the corpses to his neighbor, Mrs. Lovett, to use in her meat pies.

Though the legend usually depicts Todd as a villain, this musical version is based on a dramatization that made Sweeney a victim of perverted justice. Sondheim was the catalyst for this project, and as directed by Harold Prince, this *Sweeney* took no prisoners and spared no sensibilities. Perhaps the supreme achievement of the show—other than its breathtaking virtuosity—is the humanizing effect the authors have on the two central characters—Mrs. Lovett is a lovelorn capitalist, while Todd himself emerges a wronged husband and father driven to madness.

2. ***THE NEWS***

This small-scale musical, which was booked in the Helen Hayes—the smallest theater on Broadway—still seemed too small for the Main Stem, and it unfortunately shows up on many "Worst of the '80s" lists. It's a rock-opera semi-satire on the methods and madness of a tabloid newspaper, in particular their treatment of a serial killer on their front pages.

Critics were united in their dislike for *The News*, which seemed to have no real handle on its subject matter, trivializing both the paper (which bore a masthead resemblance to a certain paper rhyming with "You Pork Ghost") and the serial killer who winds up dating the editor's daughter. Mostly the work of Paul Schierhorn, who was nominated for two Tony awards for this four-performance flop, *The News* was mostly sung, and a good thing, too: Coming in for most of the credit were Cheryl Alexander as a reporter and future Tony winner Anthony Crivello as the killer.

3. ***LITTLE SHOP OF HORRORS***

The enjoyable musical setting of Roger Corman's zero-budget horror film *The Little Shop of Horrors*. In movie and musical, nerdy Seymour tends the cannibalistic plant Audrey II (named for his boss's daughter, the object of Seymour's affections). As Audrey II grows, her appetite for human blood grows as well, and Seymour must feed his plant or suffer the consequences.

A huge off-Broadway hit (by Alan Menken and

Howard Ashman), which was subsequently made into a successful and stylish film, *Little Shop* told its tale in 50's shoo-bop style, with a Greek-chorus-like trio of girl singers (cleverly named Chiffon, Crystal, and Ronnette, after the girl groups of the period) guiding us through the action.

4. *assassins*

Stephen Sondheim's dark side strikes again! With the misery index nearing an all-time high, and the country suffering through a recession and a controversial war, Playwrights Horizons in Manhattan presented Sondheim's *Assassins* off-Broadway in the winter of 1991. Critics were divided, with most enjoying the score but not the concept.

A bleak look at those unhappy folks who assassinated, or at least tried to kill a U.S. President, Sondheim and librettist John Weidman saw them as a sort of loser's club of Americana, with every member having a story to tell. Sondheim excelled here, presenting these historical characters through the time in which they lived (a Coplandesque folk ballad for "pioneer" John Wilkes Booth, a Carpenters parody for would-be assassins John Hinckley and Squeaky Fromme), using the pastiche as both biting commentary and superb story-telling.

5. *LEGS DIAMOND*

One of the most notorious flop shows of the '80s, *Legs Diamond* made the twin mistakes of trying to musicalize the story of a gangster and then trying to use his desire for a showbiz career as an excuse for his criminal activity. The bomb detonated on the stage of the Mark Hellinger Theater was so huge it took the power of a higher being to rescue it, as the Times Square Gospel Church took over the theater after *Legs* ran away.

The great playwright Harvey Fierstein was partially responsible for the book, which aimed for Runyonesque color and grit but had too much unintentional gay camp beneath the surface. Cabaret performer and recording artist Peter Allen wrote the score and played the title role. He was unconvincing both as the songwriter and as the titular gangster and lothario.

6. *THE CAPEMAN*

Legendary songwriter Paul Simon's ill-starred musical, based on a true story a 1959 murder in the streets of New York City. The piece, despite noble intentions, was never convincingly theatrical, and many critics called it cantata-like, citing a lack of a coherent stage motor to drive it.

Sixteen-year-old Salvador Agron knifed two innocent men when his gang, the Vampires, went looking for the Irish gang the Norsemen. (Agron was identified by witnesses by his red and black cape, hence the nickname.) Agron's life and times (sentenced to death, his sentence was commuted, and he served 20 years), which might have made a stunning musical, were unfortunately somewhat trivialized.

7. *THOU SHALT NOT*

This 2002 quasi-glamour project, created by hot director-choreographer Susan Stroman and even hotter composer-lyricist Harry Connick, Jr., was a musical adaptation of Emile Zola's novel *Thérèse Raquin*. The result, despite the pedigrees of its creators, was an unfocused, often troubled show with moments of quality.

The musical followed Zola's plot closely, but switched

Singer-songwriter-heartthrob Harry Connick, Jr. made
it to Broadway as a composer in 2002 with the dark murder tale
Thou Shalt Not.

the action from Europe to post-war N'awlins, allowing Connick to indulge his Southern jazz roots by writing a steamy score. Stroman's work was very dance-heavy; this talented choreographer seemed to fall back on the weak libretto band-aid of extraneous dance. Of the cast, most of the plaudits went to Norbert Leo Butz, as Thérèse's schlubby husband Camille, who was ultimately driven to rage by his wife's betrayal.

8. *MARIE CHRISTINE*

As a showcase for the remarkably talented Audra McDonald, this 1999 Michael John LaChiusa musical was pretty successful. In most other respects, *Marie Christine* was less so. This musical retelling of the *Medea* tale starred McDonald as the doomed wife and mother of the title, driven by her passions and the prejudices of the day. Like the aforementioned *Thou Shalt Not*, *Marie Christine* reset its classic tale in steamy, sensuous New Orleans.

LaChiusa and director Graciela Daniele reset the action in the 1890s, in Chicago as well as New Orleans, where Marie was a Creole fascinated with the mysteries of voodoo. LaChiusa's score veered from lyrical to wildly hysterical—unfortunately, mostly the latter.

9. *PARADE*

Parade was a critically lauded but commercially unsuccessful 1999 Lincoln Center musical based on the murder of Mary Phagan, a young Georgia girl, in 1913. The crime was pinned on her factory foreman, a transplanted New York Jew named Leo Frank, whose trial was, to put it mildly, biased. Ultimately, the show became a story of strength under duress.

Musicalizing this story was tricky, and librettist Alfred Uhry, composer/lyricist Jason Robert Brown, and director Harold Prince delivered a dark, nuanced show that focused mostly on the relationship between Frank and his wife, Lucille. Brown in particular was able to wed the many musical styles native to the time (spirituals, rags, marches) to character development, using a chain-gang call-and-response, for instance, when the Governor of Georgia visits a prison farm to interrogate a key witness.

10. *JACK'S HOLIDAY*

This very unfulfilling off-Broadway musical tale about Jack the Ripper journeying to America lasted only twenty-five performances when produced at Playwrights Horizons in 1995. As is the case with many shows in this fanciful vein, the authors, who apparently didn't trust their source material enough, used show business as a plot device.

Jack's Holiday, written by Mark St. Germain and Randy Courts, floats the notion that the notorious London Ripper came to New York in 1892 as part of a visiting theater troupe (uh-huh), supposedly because the evils of New York were worse than those he left behind in England. Well, judging by this flop, the theater must be better in England, anyway. Despite overwhelmingly negative reviews, some praise was heard for Judy Blazer as Irish whore Mary Healey, and also for Jerome Sirlin's clever sets and projections.

Every Movie's a Circus

10 Legendary Broadway Performers Who Lost Their Roles in the Movie Version

E very so often, a performer comes along who creates an indelible, definitive performance in a Broadway musical . . . and then sees the role given to an established star for the movie version. In most cases, the movie performer can't even compare with what a great stage performer would have brought to the role. Here are ten stage actors who lost it to the movies.

1. **RICHARD KILEY, *Man of La Mancha***

Miguel Cervantes' classic novel *Don Quixote* was superbly adapted, in 1965, into *Man of La Mancha*, and part of the genius of the show is the conceit of putting Cervantes on stage to defend his manuscript in a kangaroo court of prison inmates. He then proceeds to tell the tale of Don Quixote de La Mancha, and becomes Quixote himself.

Less cynical and more inspirational (and therefore more in tune with the flower-power era that was on the rise) than the novel, *Man of La Mancha* requires a lead actor with the bravura to portray a noble author, a driven knight-errant, and the dying fool he becomes. That actor is Richard Kiley, who gave one of the most commanding performances in musical theater history, winning raves even from critics who dismissed the show as vulgar, and cleaning up at awards time. Naturally, he'd carry over in the movie version, right? Wrong. Peter O'Toole was tapped to play Quixote in the movie version, and while O'Toole is a commanding actor, his Quixote doesn't sing *or* tilt at windmills as movingly as Kiley did on stage.

2. JULIE ANDREWS, *MY FAIR LADY*

Julie Andrews entranced Broadway in a featured role in Sandy Wilson's *The Boy Friend* in 1954, and after Mary Martin said no, Andrews outlasted all others to win the role of "squashed cabbage leaf" Eliza Doolittle in *My Lady Liza*. By the time it had become *My Fair Lady* in 1956, the show and its leading lady were pretty much invincible. An almost unprecedented smash hit on Broadway and in London, *My Fair Lady* had movie-musical fans and Julie-worshippers drooling in anticipation of the big-screen version.

Now comes the hairy part. Andrews was not considered a sufficient box office draw in 1963, when *My Fair Lady* was filmed, so the part went to the impossibly glamorous, yet mousy, Audrey Hepburn. Some have speculated that while Hepburn may not have been ideal (particularly in the first half), she projected more vulnerability onscreen than Andrews might have, and that's why Jack Warner went with Hepburn. The well-known upshot of all this hoo-ha is that ultimately, while *My Fair Lady* won a slew of Oscars, including Best Picture, Andrews won the Best Actress Oscar for *Mary Poppins*, in which she was marvelous, but about as vulnerable as the Great Wall of China. Hepburn, of course, didn't sing most of her songs and got no Oscar nomination.

3. CAROL CHANNING, *HELLO, DOLLY!*

If any Broadway performer is more identified with a role than Kiley or Andrews, it must be Carol Channing, who, after triumphing as Lorelei Lee in 1949's *Gentlemen Prefer Blondes*, scored as the one and only Dolly Gallagher Levi in *Hello, Dolly!* in 1964. Setting Broadway on its ear like no performer since, it was only natural that she play Dolly in the 1969 movie . . .

OK, you know it went to Barbra Streisand.

Younger, and singularly popular in movie musicals at the time, Streisand was still not up to the giddy, clickety-clack weirdness of Dolly Levi, whom she played as a quick-talking, steamrolling Yenta, much the same way she would play Judy Maxwell in Peter Bogdanovich's *What's Up, Doc?* three years later. Think of the scene in the Harmonia Gardens Restaurant, where Streisand eats roast chicken and dumplings (and dumplings and dumplings). Now imagine Channing doing it, that wide red mouth, those button eyes, that blond wig hosting a family of peacocks. It was a smash moment on stage, it would have won her the Oscar in close-up on film.

But just as she lost Lorelei Lee to the icon of the '50s, Marilyn Monroe, she lost Dolly Levi to the icon of the '60s, Barbra Streisand. Through it all, she retained her class and good humor, which is why she could still successfully tour *Hello, Dolly!* into the '90s.

4. ETHEL MERMAN, *GYPSY*

Ethel Merman capped her career with the fascinatingly repellent (repellently fascinating?) Rose in this Jule Styne–Stephen Sondheim–Arthur Laurents 1959 masterpiece, belting out classics like "Everything's Coming Up Roses," "You'll Never get Away From Me," and the horrific, purgative "Rose's Turn."

Since Merman never made much of an impact in movies (exception—*It's a Mad Mad Mad Mad World*—wow!), the double takes were small (except Merman's, who was reportedly promised the role early and often) when Rosalind Russell signed to play Rose in the 1962 Mervyn LeRoy film. *Gypsy* on film is fairly faithful to its brilliant stage origins, and Russell gives it her professional best (with her singing dubbed by the similarly throaty Lisa Kirk). But if you've heard Merman rip through the score, you realize how much she's missed, and how much LeRoy missed the opportunity to turn one of the best book musicals ever into one of the best film musicals ever.

5. ANGELA LANSBURY, *MAME*

For Rosalind Russell, before there was Rose, there was *Auntie Mame*. Russell triumphed in the stage and film versions of the Patrick Dennis memoir, but was never considered for the inevitable musical version. And after many leading ladies *were* considered, the part fell to Angela Lansbury, who had surprised audiences with her fine singing in *Anyone Can Whistle* in 1964. As directed by Gene Saks, and co-starring seven thousand costumes, Lansbury seemed the very reincarnation of the irrepressible Mame Dennis Burnside. Hers was a Star Performance in every sense of the word, with the

1966 Tony Award and dressing-room worshippers to follow.

So why, oh why, did the property languish for eight years? And who, who, *WHO* thought Lucille Ball was right for the part of Mame at age 63? It had been proven that Ball couldn't really sing, thirteen years earlier, in *Wildcat*. But by 1974, she was just plain too old (Lansbury was 48, just right) and just plain too "sitcom Mom" for the force of nature that was Mame. Mame is *not* a mother, that's the point. Lucille Ball, after playing three sitcom Moms in succession on TV, fell flat.

6. ZERO MOSTEL, *FIDDLER ON THE ROOF*

After Zero Mostel hit huge with his Papa Tevye in Broadway's *Fiddler on the Roof*, he made six movies (including the awful version of *A Funny Thing Happened on the Way to the Forum*) and cemented his reputation as a brilliant, egomaniacal manchild. When it finally came time to turn *Fiddler* into a movie, however, his difficulties weighed less against him than the fact that he was considered too "big," too unreal, for the unforgiving camera. (One look at him stretching the fabric of *The Producers* should convince anyone of that.)

Mostel was predictably, operatically, crushed when producer Walter Mirisch gave the role to Topol, the Israeli actor who had played Tevye with success in London and elsewhere. The film version of *Fiddler* won raves and Oscars (Topol received a nomination, but lost to Gene Hackman, for the decidedly non-musical *The French Connection*) but was opened up and "realized," as most movie musicals eventually are. Off the stage, and without Boris Aronson's beautiful, stylized,

Chagall-like sets, perhaps the overpowering Mostel would have been inappropriate.

7. DOROTHY LOUDON, *annie*

The well-crafted and touching *Annie* was a smash-hit success, and much of that success was due to its leads: Andrea McArdle, who stepped into the role of the Little Orphan when the first-choice girl wasn't working out; Reid Shelton, gruff but lovable as Daddy Warbucks; and the awesome Dorothy Loudon as Miss Hannigan, the sweet-like-a-molotov-cocktail orphanage head-mistress.

The comic villainess is a staple of musical comedy, and Dorothy Loudon has played many of them in her great career. But after a few flops in the '60s, she got her big chance with Miss Hannigan, who rides herd over her orphans in Act One and schemes to usurp Warbucks' fortune in Act Two. Hannigan is a character co-medienne's dream come true, with great dialogue and a fabulous "want" number called "Easy Street," and Loudon bit fiercely into the role and deservedly won a Tony Award. But Loudon, as fine a performer as she is, is not a household name, and since kids and parents across America was waiting for the movie version, it wasn't really a shock when she lost the role.

The movie version of *Annie* was directed by John Huston, and yes, that's what everyone thought: *John Huston*? John "We don't need no stinking badges" Huston? Decidedly unsentimental is one thing, but mercy. He put too much back in the movie (like the unnecessary Punjab and The Asp, from the comic strip), but at least he got this right: He got Carol Burnett for Miss Hannigan. If it's true that Loudon wouldn't have sold the movie, Burnett is pretty much the TV-and-movies version of Dorothy Loudon, a high-octane, do-anything tornado with enough belt to keep the chorus boys' pants up.

8. **PATTI LuPONE,** *EVITA*

Patti LuPone had been steadily working in New York for several years, much of that time as a member of John Houseman's Acting Company, when she starred in Harold Prince's production of the Rice/Lloyd Webber *Evita* in 1979. When London's Evita, Elaine Paige, was denied the opportunity to recreate the role in New York, names as diverse as Raquel Welch (hmm), Ann-Margret (MMM), and Charo (koochy!) were bandied about by the press. Eventually, LuPone took the role, and when Prince toned down the Fascist-rally overtones of the London production, it fell to LuPone to supply much of the ferocity inherent in the ruthless social climber who became First Lady of Argentina, presumably, according to Rice and Lloyd Webber, through sheer will. LuPone was indeed ferocious, and she wowed even the critics who disliked the show, winning the Tony Award and becoming a huge star.

That LuPone never played *Evita* on film is not entirely her fault. The property kicked around Hollywood longer than a Busby Berkeley chorus line, and by the time the cameras rolled in 1995, everyone from Meryl Streep to Barbra Streisand had been mentioned. The part finally fell to the most obvious choice, the one and only Madonna.

Madonna's participation in the film and the attendant hysteria surrounding it were nevertheless the most measured things about Alan Parker's overblown, tarted-up movie version of *Evita*. (Actually, put Jonathan Pryce's Juan Perón in the "measured" category, too.)

Unfortunately, by the mid-90s, LuPone was simply too old and didn't possess the screen glamour necessary to carry a film version of *Evita*, especially one as terminally stupid as Parker's.

9.   **MARY MARTIN,** *THE SOUND OF MUSIC*

There was a stage version of *The Sound of Music*? Indeed there was, sonny, and it bears some resemblance to the movie, though not as much as you'd think. Chiefly, it wasn't the fully integrated Rodgers and Hammerstein musical play that it had been on the stage. It became, instead, a Julie Andrews Movie. This made perfect sense, considering when the movie was made, but before Julie Andrews on film, there was Mary Martin on stage.

Mary Martin, the charming, lighthearted heroine of many a musical smash, created the role of Maria Von Trapp in *The Sound of Music* in 1959, besting Ethel Merman (*Gypsy*) and Carol Burnett (*Once Upon a Mattress*) in the Tony Awards race that season, which should have been enough to win her the film role right there. But as even her supporters pointed out, she was too old to have even played Maria on stage, and the camera would have been unforgiving. Not that, at 50-something, she was any bad shakes to look at, but still . . .

Julie Andrews, on the other hand, was 22 years Mary Martin's junior, just as entrancing a musical performer, and, incidentally, the hottest movie star in the world, having just won the Oscar for *Mary Poppins* the year before. So when even the film editor said "when in doubt, cut to Julie Andrews," it was pretty obvious that Andrews had become a legitimate phenomenon. Rodgers liked her so much that, following Hammerstein's death, he penned Andrews a new song, "I Have Confidence," that the Martin Maria probably would have never sung. But as Andrews was a Sherman tank of confidence on camera, it worked perfectly to set her character up for the balance of the film.

10. CHITA RIVERA, *BYE BYE BIRDIE*

Upon her triumphant return to Broadway in 1993's *Kiss of the Spider Woman*, the phenomenal Chita Rivera was asked by a TV reporter why she hadn't done more film work. Her answer was simple: "Darling, no one ever asked me."

Two of the great ironies of the musical theater are that Chita Rivera had to wait so long for a Tony (1984), and that she never made more movies. But Miss Dolores Conchita Figueroa del Rivero has always been one of Broadway's most admired leading ladies, an incomparable triple threat who added a spark of Latin passion to a post-Eisenhower Golden Age Broadway. Her performance as long-suffering Rose in *Bye Bye Birdie*, which found her doing good comedy as well as dancing the floor off, was a highlight of an already superb show, an examination of the approaching Rock era and its bewildering effects on parents and their children. The movie version, however, was a different story.

Rose, as written to be played by Janet Leigh, was stripped of her ethnic heritage (yet named Rose De Leon, go figure Hollywood), so Rivera, not exactly box-office dynamite in Tinseltown, was dispensable. So why did they put Leigh in a black wig and make her up dark? As an apology to Rivera-lovers? Almost everything about the movie is wrong, except Dick Van Dyke and Paul Lynde, reprising their original performances, but the omission of Rivera clinches mediocre status for the film.

Rivera and Van Dyke had tremendous chemistry on stage; indeed, that's why the show ends with Albert and Rose in each other's arms, and not with the high-schoolers Kim and Hugo. The movie ends with the in-appropriate Ann-Margret (yeah, what a sweet high-school kid, huh?) belting out the forgettable new title song. That's what Janet Leigh meant to the film.

I Think I Can Play This Part

10 Broadway Performers Who Did the Movie Version

F ew movie musicals have ever lived up to their predecessors in terms of quality. In many cases, it's because producers courted a certain star who simply turned out wrong for the big part. Here are ten performers who rightly got a shot at recreating their Broadway triumphs on film.

1. **JOEL GREY,** *CABARET*

Cabaret's grotesquely rouged-up, evil-clown Emcee was chillingly embodied by Joel Grey, playing host to the patrons of the Kit Kat Klub as well as ironic commentator on the fascism beating down the door of the Klub, and, by extension, all Germany. The Emcee's presence at the fringes was more terrifying than the show's more overt Nazi bullyboys, and Grey won a Featured Actor Tony in 1966.

Bob Fosse's 1972 film version of *Cabaret*, quite a different animal than the stage version, offers its own considerable pleasures, and chief among them is Grey. Essaying the Emcee again, he is more omnipresent, more malevolent, and less charming (if possible) than he was onstage, but just as memorable. He was awarded the Best Supporting Actor Academy Award for his work in the film version.

2. **ROBERT PRESTON,** *THE MUSIC MAN*

It bears repeating that before Meredith Willson's *The Music Man*, Robert Preston was often cast as a hard guy or a clergyman, both on stage and on screen. Harold Hill, lightfooted but shady salesman, was neither heavy nor heavenly, but Preston took to musical theater like a duck to water. It was inevitable that he would star in the film version of *The Music Man*, as he was an established screen presence at the time.

Morton Da Costa directed Preston in both the stage and screen versions of *The Music Man*, and though the film is a bit stagy, Preston is not. His charisma and charm burn through the screen.

3. **JUDY HOLLIDAY,** *BELLS ARE RINGING*

Bells are Ringing, a pleasant enough musical comedy, was set aloft by the radiance and appeal of Judy Holliday's performance as Ella Peterson, Susanswerphone girl. Holliday received love letters from both crowds and critics, and stayed with the show through its entire 924-performance run.

Librettists and lyricists Betty Comden and Adolph Green had conceived *Bells are Ringing* for their friend Holliday, and her legendary Tony-winning performance ensured Holliday would play Ella on screen. Although the movie disappointed, she didn't, projecting both her sweet vulnerability and her facility with a throwaway line.

4. **WILLIAM DANIELS, *1776***

Although *1776* is basically a well-made musical play for a superb male ensemble, John Adams is definitely the starring role. And John Adams, as written by Peter Stone and Sherman Edwards, was thrillingly embodied by the abrasive yet engaging William Daniels.

Much of the original Broadway cast of this unlikely hit recreated their roles on film, Daniels included. While the film has its weak moments, Daniels manages to duplicate the balancing act he achieved on stage, making us root for his cause while wishing he would just shut up, already.

5. **BARBRA STREISAND, *FUNNY GIRL***

It was bound to happen: Carol Channing conquered Barbra Streisand on Broadway, so Barbra Streisand naturally felt she had to conquer the world (and, incidentally, Carol Channing). Streisand blazed to superstardom in *Funny Girl*, the Jule Styne–Bob Merrill–Isobel Lennart musical bio of the legendary comedienne Fanny Brice. But Channing, as Dolly, bested her in the Tony race that year. So Streisand looked in a mirror and said, "Someday I will control the universe."

Producer Ray Stark had always imagined *Funny Girl* as a screen property, so giving Streisand the film was academic. Seldom has a performer been as self-assured as Streisand was in *Funny Girl*. So she knocked everybody's socks off and won the Oscar in 1968. (Tied with Katharine Hepburn, actually.) She had her pick of roles after that, and she chose *Hello, Dolly!* and finally trumped La Channing.

6. **YUL BRYNNER, *THE KING AND I***

Another impossibility: Imagine this movie without Yul Brynner. A puzzlement, yes? Did Yul Brynner ever play any other role than the King of Siam, anyway? Well, yes, roughly fifty of them, but King Mongkut was undeniably his supreme creation.

On stage, the King was a supporting role to Anna Leonowens, created for Gertrude Lawrence. But after Brynner triumphed in the show on Broadway, the film version became much more Brynner-riffic, due to the Russian's exotic on-camera appeal (and, incidentally, the absence of Lawrence). After the Academy Award, he never had a major stage triumph that didn't involve the King.

7.   ROBERT MORSE, *HOW TO SUCCEED IN BUSINESS WITHOUT REALLY TRYING*

The role of J. Pierrepont Finch is one of the juiciest in all of musical comedy, and Robert Morse became a huge star thanks to his portrayal of the ravenous corporate climber. *How to Succeed . . .* won the Tony and the Pulitzer, and Morse eagerly signed on for the film version.

Unfortunately, much of the great Frank Loesser score is excised from the film version, and the cartoony look and style of the original production is also lost on the big screen. But Morse is in fine form, his mannerisms and charm on display throughout the piece, and he's paired well with the beautiful Michele Lee, who took over the role of Rosemary from Bonnie Scott on Broadway. Also seen to good advantage are the priceless Rudy Vallee as Biggley, and Ruth Kobart as Jonesy, his secretary, both from Broadway as well. But it's Morse's show and movie all the way.

8.   GWEN VERDON, *DAMN YANKEES*

Whatever Lola wants, Lola gets, and Gewen Verdon got tons of critical praise (not to mention a bushel and a

peck of whoops and hollers from the tired businessmen) for her portrayal of Lola, a minion of the Devil
who can ruin any man. The 1955 stage version of
Damn Yankees cemented her reputation as a triple
threat with sex appeal, but the film version of the musical, she comes across less well, as her immediacy and
sexiness are lost on the screen. As riveting as Verdon
was live, she's unfortunately only so-so on film.

9. PETER PALMER, *LI'L ABNER*

On film, *Li'l Abner* is one of the most faithful and satisfying recreations of a stage musical ever seen. Adding
to the fun in *Li'l Abner* is the casting of physical types
to fill out Al Capp's demented comic strip worldview.
And no one could inhabit the physique of man-child
Abner Yokum better than Peter Palmer.

Palmer was, as is obvious to anyone who's ever
seen him, a football player before he became a Broadway actor, but he was a natural charmer. Despite false
alarms (Rock Hudson was out front one night, scaring
Palmer to death), Palmer was flown to Hollywood,
tested, and landed the role of Abner in the film version,
with his reviews mostly of the "lovable lunkhead" variety.

10. ELLEN GREENE, LITTLE SHOP OF HORRORS

When your first Broadway job is the calamitous *Rachael Lily Rosenbloom*, there's nowhere to go but up.
And up went Ellen Greene, a superb singing comedienne who landed her signature role, Audrey in *Little
Shop of Horrors*, in 1982.

Audrey, as written by Alan Menken and Howard
Ashman, is a breathy, busty, Marilyn Monroe type who
longs for serenity and escape from the big city. Her two

big numbers couldn't be more different. Greene sweetly sold her "want" song, "Somewhere That's Green," in the first act, then ripped into the soulful gospel of the eleven o'clock number, "Suddenly Seymour." It's fitting that the only performer chosen to re-create their role in the big screen transfer of *Little Shop of Horrors* was Ellen Greene.

All Hail the Political Honeymoon

10 Musicals about Politics and Politicians

Political satire is as old as the theater itself; audiences love to marvel and/or laugh at world leaders from the safe distance of a theater seat. Here are ten political musicals that gave their audiences a stumping good time.

1. *FIORELLO!*

The first hit show from Jerry Bock and Sheldon Harnick, this bright and brassy Tony- and Pulitzer-winning musical from 1959 was a warts-and-all portrait of the Little Flower, New York City's irascible Mayor Fiorello H. LaGuardia, and the post-Tammany era which saw him shoot to political stardom.

Tom Bosley shot to stardom as LaGuardia, giving full voice to librettist Jerome Weidman's portrait of the Mayor as a loudmouthed enemy of corruption and champion of the Little Guy (and, remember, a Republican). One good reason for LaGuardia's success was his common touch: LaGuardia spoke three languages, English and the musically serendipitous Italian and Yiddish, which served as a fantastic jumping-off point for the show's big production number, a stump-speech triptych called "The Name's LaGuardia."

2. *OF THEE I SING*

"Wintergreen for President!" was the rallying cry in this immortal 1931 musical. John P. Wintergreen, that is, was candidate for office, and his running mate was Alexander Throttlebottom. The brothers Gershwin and librettists George S. Kaufman and Morrie Ryskind told a huge, quasi-comic-operatic tale in brilliantly musicalized satire, with the candidate picking a bride from a beauty contest (then refusing to marry her because she can't bake) and sweeping scenes of conventioneering and campaigning.

Easily the most structurally integrated musical of its time, it became the first tuner to win the Pulitzer Prize for drama. The idea of giving the award to a musical was so new and unexpected, however, that the prize went only to Kaufman and Ryskind. *Of Thee I Sing* was followed by a less successful (and possibly even more bizarre) sequel, *Let 'Em Eat Cake.*

3. *EVITA*

After turning Jesus into a rock star in the early '70s, Tim Rice and Andrew Lloyd Webber chose to do the same for Argentina's legendary First Lady. Rice had long been fascinated by the blonde actress who married General Juan Peron and rose to iconic status after Peron assumed the Presidency. (For his part, Webber hated her, but a job's a job.)

The politics of the era were given short shrift, mostly declared rather than musicalized or dramatized. But in the case of one number in particular, "The Art of the Possible," Prince cleverly staged the politics. Peron and three other generals describe the easiest way to make it to the top of the heap (travel the path of least resistance) as their rocking chairs disappear one by one, leaving Peron the last man standing.

A studio recording was released prior to the stage production in England, with pop stars guaranteeing the hit status of the show. Harold Prince's neo-Brechtian production was aided greatly by Elaine Paige in London and Patti LuPone in New York, both of whom offered searing depictions of this ruthless angel.

4. *I'D RATHER BE RIGHT*

The great showman George M. Cohan was lured out of semi-retirement to take a shot at portraying FDR in this 1937 Rodgers and Hart satire. Due to the popularity of the creators (Kaufman-Hart libretto) and the novelty of the casting, anticipation was almost unprecedented. And, as is almost always the result in that case, the outcome disappointed.

Cohan, despite his quarrelsome nature during rehearsals, won raves and could have run for President himself. But the show, rightly or not, was inevitably compared to *Of Thee I Sing* and found wanting. Too satirical, the critics said. Too critical, too broad. Cohan, for his part, probably said something like, "Say, listen, see?" Or was that Cagney?

5. *STRIKE UP THE BAND*

This superbly funny 1930 Gershwin brothers musical betrays the cynical streak evident in their "Wintergreen" shows, as the United States goes to war with Switzerland over cheese. It was originally conceived as a bitterly satiric anti-war tract, written by George S.

Kaufman, culminating in impending war against the Soviets. Morrie Ryskind revised Kaufman's libretto, substituting the neutral Swiss for the Reds, pointing up the satire by placing all within the context of a dream.

Hailed as not only funny and tuneful (the rescued "I've Got a Crush on You" and the title tune, which isn't really the flag-waver it has become in our time) but also intelligent, the show had a run as bittersweet as Swiss chocolate—only 191 performances. Due to the superb score, the show continues to thrive in stock and amateur productions, often sporting watered-down political content.

6. *JOHNNY JOHNSON*

The great Kurt Weill collaborated with the Group Theater's Paul Green on this anti-war *zeitoper* (a German term meaning "opera for the spirit of the times") from 1936, which examined the after-effects of World War I on a small-town lad, the eponymous Johnny.

Young Johnson tells a harrowing tale of war, of meeting an enemy soldier (also called Johnny) as pacifist as he, and of returning home, only to be hospitalized "for his own good" and turned into a street peddler. The sophisticated score played interestingly off the very uneven satire of the book, which echoed Weill's old partner, Bertolt Brecht.

7. *MAYOR*

"How'm I doin'?" was the rhetorical question Mayor Ed Koch asked of the people of New York. He also asked it in print, in his 1984 quasi-auto-biography *Mayor*, which was quickly adapted into the cabaret musical of the same title in 1985.

Featuring a book by Warren Leight (who would go

on to pen the 1999 Tony-winning play *Side Man*) and a score by the talented composer Charles Strouse, *Mayor* was a small, sketch-type show that tended to flatter Hizzoner Koch and played up his strengths as a man of the people, a mover and shaker, and a publicity hound.

8. *KNICKERBOCKER HOLIDAY*

Another Kurt Weill *zeitoper*, this anti-fascist tract from 1938 was authored by Maxwell Anderson, adapted from Washington Irving's novel *Old Knickerbocker's Guide to New York* (and featured Irving himself, commenting on the progress of the musical). Originally a critique of Franklin Delano Roosevelt, the show eventually told of Brom Broeck, the first American, so called because he wouldn't take orders from New Amsterdam's tyrannical Dutch governor, Pieter Stuyvesant.

Trouble was, Anderson's didactic book succeeded only in making his points early and too often. Weill's great score, featuring the classic "September Song," the Depression-era rouser "There's Nowhere to Go But Up," and the haunting "Requiem for a Soldier," was left to pick up the slack. *Knickerbocker Holiday* is credited as being the first musical to use a historical figure from past history to comment on present political affairs.

9. *THE FIX*

This regional theater offering was presented by the Signature Theater Company of Arlington, Virginia, in the Spring of 1998, after London's Donmar Warehouse premiered it in 1997. A modern, very dark tale of corruption, dirty politics, and murder, it featured a book and lyrics by John Dempsey, and music by Dana P. Rowe.

The Fix concerns the Chandler (Kennedy?) family, the patriarch of which dies in bed with his mistress at the show's start. The games go on from there. The scion, Cal, must keep his kinks in check and the family's skeletons in the closet in order to rise up the ladder of public office. *The Fix* earned points for its unremittingly bleak outlook.

10. **1776**

A different kind of political musical, this 1969 musical took the seminal moment in America's history, the signing of the Declaration of Independence, and brilliantly fleshed it out. As many have noted, the success of the show lay in the tension created despite the familiarity of the outcome.

1776 featured a John Adams as obnoxious and unpopular as he was brilliant and single-minded, intent on uniting the Colonies by himself, if need be. His opposition is nearly everyone else present at the Continental Congress, sweltering in the summer heat and arguing with Adams at almost every turn. Sherman Edwards' unusual yet effective score shone, particularly the song "Momma, Look Sharp," in which a soldier recounts how his best friend was shot in the field.

Peter Stone's book is a model of construction, offering a superb document to history while providing the necessary tension, most notably in a twenty-plus minute scene without music which in which the vital matters of independence are debated by all. The egalitarian integration of score, book, and staging (by Peter Hunt), as well as superb performances, made *1776* the smash hit of the season, winning the Tony for Best Musical.

Don't Fence Me In

10 Rootin' Tootin'
Western Musicals

M ost Broadway playhouses are in the West Forties (west of Broadway, that is). Here are ten musicals that gazed just a bit further west, beyond the Hudson.

1. *CRAZY FOR YOU*

A new musical (1992) loosely fashioned from the Gershwin brothers's *Girl Crazy* (1930). In both, a man heads West to the desert, and falls in love with the only girl in Deadrock, Nevada. The creators of *Crazy For You* wisely wrote a new book with palatable show-biz elements: Our hero is a wannabe hoofer who revitalizes the playhouse in town, bringing in a Follies show and reviving the spirits of the townsfolk. The Gershwin numbers were aided tremendously by choreographer Susan Stroman.

2. *DESTRY RIDES AGAIN*

James Stewart played Destry, a sheriff so effective that he tames the West without using a gun, on film in 1937's *Destry Rides Again*. The role was entrusted to

Andy Griffith for the 1959 Broadway musical version, also called *Destry Rides Again*. Produced by David Merrick (who opined that at the time there had never been a real rip-snorter of a Western musical), the score was by the estimable Harold Rome, with a book by Leonard Gershe.

3. *WILDCAT*

Cy Coleman and Carolyn Leigh wrote the score to N. Richard Nash's libretto about a hot-cha oil prospector in 1912. What made it noteworthy was the presence of Lucille Ball, in her only Broadway musical. Despite a typically fine Coleman-Leigh score (including "Hey, Look Me Over!" and "Give a Little Whistle"), the book was not distinguished, and Ball was uncomfortable (and unhealthy) throughout. It was a flop at just 172 performances and didn't last the 1960 season.

4. *OKLAHOMA!*

The landmark 1943 musical based on Lynn Riggs's 1931 play *Green Grow the Lilacs*. The plot means little (I hate you, I love you, you goin' to the dance?), but the telling is everything: cowboys, farmers, and their women all coming of age as the nation grows up around them, while Oklahoma territory becomes a state. Rodgers and Hammerstein carved their niche in the American consciousness with this classic show, the first real musical play.

5. *110 IN THE SHADE*

N. Richard Nash wrote the book for the flop *Wildcat*; it resembles his play *The Rainmaker*. Nash finally got around to adapting the play into a musical, *110 in the*

Shade, in 1963. Tom Jones and Harvey Schmidt, red-hot from *The Fantasticks*, scored the show, which concerns the men of the Curry family, their spinster sister, and the flashy fraud who finally makes all their dreams come true. The elemental trappings of the Western locale suited Jones and Schmidt; their work is typically excellent.

6. *THE WILL ROGERS FOLLIES*

It always takes place Tonight, On The Stage Of This Theater, but this1991 Tony-winning musical warmly recalls the era and the essence of America's cowboy philosopher. Director-choreographer Tommy Tune conceived the evening as a giddy, hellzapoppin' Ziegfeld Follies revue, with Mr. Ziegfeld as a disembodied voice coaching Rogers along to tell his life story. Wild West Show acts elbow the girls, girls, girls for stage time, and Rogers and his life and times are genially observed all evening, until Wiley Post finally rises from his box seat and encourages Will to go flying with him.

7. *DAS BARBECU*

Yes indeedy, Wagner's *Ring* operas reset to the contemporary West. Wagner's mammoth operas are spun for gentle comedy in this off-Broadway spoof, which finds the Valkyries chasing the ring (and the dwarf) through Texas, where it winds up as a gift at a barbecue in honor of a double wedding ceremony. *Das Barbecu*, with music by Scott Warrender and book and lyrics by Jim Luigs, premiered at Goodspeed Opera House in 1993 and moved to off-Broadway in 1994, where it had the considerable benefit of a superb cast.

8. *URBAN COWBOY*

A spring opening (and closing) in 2003, *Urban Cowboy* is closely based on the John Travolta–Debra Winger movie of the same name. Young Bud and his wife, Sissy, live their lives in contemporary Houston, with much of the action centering around Gilley's Bar and that famous mechanical bull. As is the case with many new musicals, particularly those adapted from film sources, the score is a mix of old hit songs ("Could I Have This Dance," "The Devil Went Down to Georgia") and new show tunes, in this case, tunes from several composers.

9. *PAINT YOUR WAGON*

The great songwriting team of Lerner and Loewe did most of their work in a European milieu (*My Fair Lady, Brigadoon, Gigi*), but this 1951 show, their second Broadway success, is a pure Western love story. It concerns a grizzled gold prospector and his budding daughter (who can't understand why the menfolk are always pawing her) headed to California for the Rush of 1849, and her romance with a young Mexican. Don't be put off by the film version, with those singing stars, Lee Marvin and Clint Eastwood: *Paint Your Wagon* is a superb show.

10. *THE BEST LITTLE WHOREHOUSE IN TEXAS*

A posse of Texans (authors Peter Masterson and Larry L. King, composer Carol Hall, and director-choreographer Tommy Tune) created this smash 1977 musical based on the real-life pleasure-for-poultry Chicken Ranch in west Texas. Run for generations with a tacit relationship between The Madam and The Law, it's only when a ratings-hungry TV preacher gets his truss in a twist that Sheriff Ed Earl Dodd reluctantly steps in to close 'er down. Tune's cartoonish direction (i.e., cheerleaders dancing with two life-size cheerleader dolls apiece) greatly aided the no-nonsense satire of the tale.

Bring the House Down
Pop Stars Who Crossed Over to Broadway

Like movie and TV stars, pop recording artists can rejuvenate their careers, or even find a second home, in the musical theater. Here are ten singing sensations who traded the studio and concert stage for the legitimate stage.

1. **REBA McENTIRE**

One of the most popular country singers ever, Reba McEntire had crossed over to films with her performance in Rob Reiner's dreadful *North*. She played a Texas mama who sang to convince young North to join her family. She fared better with her first Broadway project, *Annie Get Your Gun.*

Other stars followed Bernadette Peters in the role of Annie Oakley in the 1999 revival, but Reba seemed to make the most sense. Not as needlessly glamorous as Susan Lucci, she also had the "country girl" authenticity to eclipse someone like Cheryl Ladd in the role. McEntire got great reviews (some saying she was better even than Peters), and her facility with the comedy paved the way to her still-running, eponymous sitcom.

2. JOEY FATONE

Heartthrob Joey Fatone and his cohorts in the boy band N*SYNC put on a lively, almost non-stop stage show with vocal and stage pyrotechnics to spare. Fatone later branched out to pure acting, landing gigs in the vanity N*SYNC film project *On The Line* and a funny character bit in *My Big Fat Greek Wedding*. He made his Broadway debut in 2002, playing filmmaker Mark Cohen, in the long-running *Rent*.

3. TONI BRAXTON

Toni Braxton, the gorgeous, soulful, Grammy-winning R & B singer, made a belated Broadway debut as heroine Belle in *Disney's Beauty and the Beast*. Taking on the role in July of 1998, Braxton used her considerable beauty and star power to charm audiences and strike another blow for color-blind casting. While it's true that beautiful songbirds like Miss Braxton will probably never lack work, the presence of a Black Belle in the Broadway arena was nevertheless a pleasing sight. She also took on the title role in Disney's *Aida* in June 2003.

4. FRENCHIE DAVIS

Frenchie Davis is a classic example of the "failing upward" school of success which is so prevalent in show business. A surefire finalist on TV's popular *American Idol*, the plus-sized Davis found her vehicle to fame had stalled after she was discovered to have posed for an adult Internet website. (*Boo, hiss!*) "Save Frenchie" petitions went out, but Fox TV executives held their ground. (*BOO, HISS!*)

Entertainment Tonight knew a good thing when it

saw one, and hired Davis as a roving reporter. (*Aww-www.*) Finally, the outsized performer landed where she belonged—in the belter-friendly smash hit *Rent.* (*Yaaaaaay!*) Unlike either of the two *American Idol* finalists, Miss Davis appears to have the vocal chops to be able to sustain a career in front of a live audience.

5. LINDA RONSTADT

In the 1970s, many rock critics bemoaned the lack of legitimate female singing talent in the ranks; their exceptions were usually Pat Benatar and Linda Ronstadt. Joseph Papp evidently thought so, too; he put Ronstadt in the Public Theater revival of Gilbert and Sullivan's *The Pirates of Penzance* in the summer of 1980. Her wide eyes fluttering with *faux*-Victorian propriety, Ronstadt's voice was stretched somewhat thin at the top of the killer role of Major-General Stanley's daughter Mabel, but her rock-star presence was one of the many offbeat delights in the successful revival. Showing off her versatility futher, Ronstadt's concert of Mexican music, *Canciones de Mi Padre*, played Broadway in the summer of 1988.

6. SEBASTIAN BACH

Dude. Skid Row lead singer Sebastian Bach has apparently found a second career in the musical theater. Admittedly, though, the roles he's found in the theater have only been a stone's throw from the role of hair band frontman. His first stint was in the long-running Wildhorn-Bricusse turkey *Jekyll & Hyde*, taking over the huge role of the titular fun couple in June of 2000. Next on his plate was Riff Raff in the revival of *The Rocky Horror Show*, which he took over just in time for Halloween in 2001. He was dismissed, amid some mystery, from 2003's national tour of *Jesus Christ Superstar*. Dude.

7. SHEENA EASTON

The bonnie Scot lassie with the number one hit made her Broadway debut in 1991, after a tour in what ads called "one of the musical theater's great sexy parts," Aldonza, in *Man of La Mancha*. (Memo to marketing: She's not. She's a "kitchen slut reeking of sweat."). Easton got pretty bad notices, but the whole revival was a wash until some old hands came in to save it, like the original Aldonza, Joan Diener. Easton could have been well-served by Broadway; she's beautiful and can act and sing, as evinced by a stint on TV's *Miami Vice*. *Brigadoon*, anyone?

8. DEBORAH GIBSON

Eighties pop moppet turns Broadway trouper! So might the headlines read for Deborah, a/k/a Debbie Gibson. The possessor of Billboard number one singles before she could drink, Miss Gibson turned to the Broadway stage not long after that, playing Eponine in *Les Miserables* in 1991, and following up with *Disney's Beauty and the Beast* (preceding Toni Braxton, as it happens), *Grease*, and, following tours of *Joseph and the Amazing Technicolor Dreamcoat, Funny Girl,* and *Gypsy* in New Jersey, she took over the star-spangled replacement reins of Sally Bowles in the Roundabout revival of *Cabaret*.

9. VANESSA WILLIAMS

Vanessa Williams is basically Frenchie Davis writ large (you should pardon the expression): Miss America, disgraced by porn photos, lays low until everyone realizes she can sing and act, carves out a huge pop career, then hits Broadway. While her beauty was obvious at first sight, Williams took her time in hitting the Main Stem, finally taking over from the great Chita Rivera in *Kiss of the Spider Woman*. That role, a mysterious Argentinian film icon, was not such a great fit, but after a good stab at another Rivera role, Rose in a TV-movie *Bye Bye Birdie*, and a triumph in a 1997 concert production of *St. Louis Woman*, she blazed back to Broadway as the Witch (sporting warts in Act One, a killer Roman wrap outfit in Act Two) in the 2002 revival of the Sondheim-Lapine *Into the Woods*.

10. CAROLE KING

One of the greatest female songwriters ever, the great Carole King carved out her own space in pop music history as both a songwriter and a superb performer. Her considerable catalogue of songs, including such all-time greats as "The Loco-Motion," "You've Got a Friend," and "Tapestry," has been excerpted in three different Broadway shows, most notoriously the 1982 disaster *Rock and Roll! The First 5,000 Years*.

King finally made her dramatic debut on Broadway in 1995, playing Mother Johnstone in Willy Russell's one-of-a-kind musical *Blood Brothers*. She took over the role of a conflicted mother of identical twins, forced to give one up at birth, from another pop star, Petula Clark.

Come Back to Me

10 Hollywood Stars Who Crossed Over to Broadway

Now, as in the past, Broadway serves as a "training ground" for many future movie and television stars. Likewise, a Hollywood star's appearance on the Main Stem can pre-sell a show or give the box office a much-needed shot in the arm. Here are ten performers who made it big in Hollywood, then played New York, often returning in triumph.

1. STING

Rock legend Sting (nee Gordon Sumner), of the band The Police, was represented on Broadway in 1982 via some Police tunes in the disastrous revue *Rock and Roll! The First 5,000 Years.* But in 1990, after rock stardom and some genuine movie acclaim, he made his Broadway acting debut as gang leader Macheath in Michael Feingold's translation of the Brecht-Weill classic, *3 Penny Opera.* The revival was not very well received, but Sting received acclaim for his performance in some circles.

2. **KATHARINE HEPBURN**

Perhaps the greatest movie actress of all time, the late, great Kate appeared in plays on Broadway as early as 1928. But it wasn't until 1969, and after several Oscars, that she made her Broadway musical debut. For Hepburn to deign to perform in a tuner, the subject had to be as legendary as she, and indeed it was: The show was *Coco*, and Hepburn wittily essayed the part of designer Coco Chanel, she of the pink suit and big glasses. (Hepburn made the scene in the big glasses, but mostly stuck to slacks.) As high-profile as her return was, she was basically playing herself, and critics and audiences loved it live. They loved her more than the show, though, and Hepburn lost the Tony Award, to . . .

3. **LAUREN BACALL**

. . . Who made her musical debut that same season, in *Applause*, the musical version of the classic film *All About Eve*. Bacall completely dug the groovy modern-day adaptation, swinging in a disco here, dishing with her gay hairdresser there, covering up her lack of real musical-theater savvy with her effortless glamour and star power. Despite the presence of Hepburn in *Coco*, just a couple of blocks north, Bacall's was by far the biggest and most heralded star turn of the season. Her next musical was over a decade later, in *Woman of the Year*, another adaptation, this time from a Tracy-Hepburn film (oh, the irony). Bacall's typical no-nonsense glamour and that unassailable star power won her another Tony, and she was later replaced in the role by . . .

4. **RAQUEL WELCH**

. . . Who took over the role of Tess Harding from Bacall
in 1982. Welch's movie career was running on fumes
at this time, but her Broadway debut created a stir of its
own, skewing the role a bit younger, and offering a very
different kind of glamour and hotness than Bacall. Predictably, the press embarrassed themselves, getting
their tongues caught in their typewriters and debating
the proper way to spell "AA-OOOOOO-GAH!"

Thirteen years later, Miss Welch played a role even
more implausible than Tess Harding, when she followed Julie Andrews into the Broadway flop *Victor/Vic-
toria*. *Myra Breckenridge* repeated itself here, as Welch,
the *ur*-female, again played a woman dabbling in sexual ambiguity.

5. **DAVID HASSELHOFF**

Say what you will about the star of *Knight Rider* and
Baywatch, he was at least partly responsible for turning the former into a household name (including a
forthcoming full-length "reunion" movie) and the latter
into the most popular TV show on the planet. Hasselhoff also enjoys a successful career as a pop star in
Germany and a decent level of fame here in the states,
so the producers of the long-running *Jekyll & Hyde*,
Frank Wildhorn, wasn't exactly whistling "Dixie" when
they asked Hasselhoff to take over the title dual roles.

For three months in 2000, Hasselhoff took on gal-
lant Henry Jekyll and goofus Mr. Hyde in Frank Wildhorn and Leslie Bricusse's cheesy take on Robert Louis
Stevenson's Victorian horror tale. TV cameras for the
Broadway Television Network recorded Hasselhoff's

last night, and although he worked hard, the high-camp, totally silly material defeated him soundly. (His karate-kick exit after his curtain call didn't help either.) Rumors have Hasselhoff headed back to Broadway in a revival of Lerner and Loewe's *Paint Your Wagon*.

6. LIZA MINNELLI

While it couldn't have been easy for a performer to grow up as Judy Garland's daughter, Liza Minnelli obviously had the talent to go the distance. Her first musical was the confusing *Flora, the Red Menace*, which did less for her than she did for the show. She did, however, win a Tony for *Flora* at age nineteen, and that show's composer and lyricist, John Kander and Fred Ebb, wrote their next score, *Cabaret*, with Minnelli in mind. She didn't do it on stage but had some mild success with the film version (you know, co-starring with a guy named Oscar!).

Movie success in other genres followed, as well as the legendary TV special *Liza With a "Z,"* and she had fully inherited her mother's legacy by this time. She often returned to Broadway, in full shows (Tony-winning *The Act* in 1977) as well as specialty engagements (like *Liza* in 1974).

7. GLENN CLOSE

Glenn Close made her Broadway debut in the play *Love for Love* in 1974; a year and a half later, she made her musical debut in Richard Rodgers's *Rex*. Close's movie career really took off after she was Tony-nominated in *Barnum*; she appeared in *The World According to Garp* not long after, and *Garp* won her the first of her five Oscar nominations. She came back to Broadway in 1983, winning a Tony for the play *The Real Thing*, again in 1992, winning her second Tony for the play *Death and the Maiden*, and won her third Tony in 1995, for her haunting Norma Desmond in Andrew Lloyd Webber's musical *Sunset Boulevard*.

8. JOHN STAMOS

Pretender to the throne of King-of-TV-Movie-Land, John Stamos is an unusual Broadway crossover star, but he's proven his chops with stints in musicals that couldn't be more different. The "stunt" casting of a TV heartthrob may have been at work, but sometimes, these things have a way of working.

Stamos, in addition to being an actor, is an accomplished percussionist (yes, he really does play congas in the Beach Boys "Kokomo" video) and singer, so his appearance as Matthew Broderick's replacement in the 1995 revival of *How to Succeed in Business Without Really Trying* was not completely out of left field. For his next Broadway gig, in the highly charged revival of *Cabaret*, he definitely didn't play it safe. In the spring of 2002, he took over the role of the androgynous, sexually suggestive Emcee for five months. Late in 2003, he got more press by stepping into the role of Guido Contini in the Broadway revival of *Nine*, succeeding the very popular Antonio Banderas.

9. BETTE DAVIS

Another candidate for Greatest Movie Star Ever, Bette Davis appeared in two musicals in her great career, with less-than-spectacular results. In 1952, she appeared, with much hoopla, in the musical *Two's Company*, but had to withdraw early because of health problems. Her early departure caused no little financial distress to the producers.

In 1964, Emlyn Williams adapted his play *The Corn is Green* into the musical *Miss Moffat*, ostensibly as a project for Mary Martin. Ten years later, *Miss Moffat* was offered to the woman who had played her on film, Bette Davis. Davis accepted a pre-Broadway tour, then the fireworks began. She proved to be less than stellar as a singer and started to miss performances, raising the red flag again with the producers. She ultimately clashed loudly with the show's director, Joshua Logan, as well. *Miss Moffat* never made it to Broadway.

10. **TOM BOSLEY**

After blazing to stardom as Mayor LaGuardia in *Fiorello!* in 1959, Tom Bosley found his good-natured bravado in some demand. Unfortunately, his next musical projects weren't up to the level of the Pulitzer-winning *Fiorello!* The first show, *Nowhere to Go but Up*, from 1962, was a subpar comic musical about Depression-era bootleggers Izzy and Moe, and his next musical, 1968's *The Education of H*Y*M*A*N K*A*P*L*A*N*, an immigrant's tale of assimilation, might have done well had it not been undone by history. On the show's opening night, Martin Luther King, Jr. was assassinated, and the news cycle in the following days left no room for *H*Y*M*A*N K*A*P*L*A* N* to build any kind of an audience.

So Bosley lit out for Hollywood, where he found his greatest success on the TV sitcom *Happy Days*. He finally made his return to Broadway in 1994, as Belle's Father in *Disney's Beauty and the Beast*. He came back again to play Herr Schultz in the revival of *Cabaret*.

It's a Hit, It's a Palpable Hit

Hit Songs You Never Knew Came from Musicals

Way back when, the music of Broadway was our nation's popular music. Every one of the ten songs below has enjoyed hit status at one time or another, but many folks don't know that these familiar melodies are actually show tunes.

1. "HE TOUCHED ME" (FROM *DRAT! THE CAT!*)

Drat! The Cat! is a sexy, funny show about an olde-tyme female jewel thief and the hapless cop who eventually catches her and wins her heart. The show, which starred Elliott Gould and Lesley Ann Warren, was a failure on Broadway in 1965, but Mr. Gould happened to be married to The Thing Itself, Barbra Streisand, and Gould's big ballad, "She Touched Me," was refashioned by Streisand and recorded as "He Touched Me." Socko, boffo, million-plus sales.

Milton Schafer and Ira Levin wrote a successfully varied score for *Drat! The Cat!,* with flat-out comedy numbers, period-style charmers, and a superb overture, but scored biggest with that hit ballad, which then reached the stratosphere when Streisand laid it down. So who knew it was written by the creator of *The Stepford Wives*?

2.   "LAZY AFTERNOON" (FROM *THE GOLDEN APPLE*)

The score to *The Golden Apple*, Jerome Moross and John LaTouche's resetting of Homer's *Iliad* and *Odyssey* in America between the years 1900–1910, is so well-integrated that it's almost impossible to imagine any part of the score standing separately from the whole. But two songs did make their way out of the score: the beautiful, wistful "Windflowers," Penelope's lament for her golden days with Ulysses, and Helen's sultry "Lazy Afternoon."

"Lazy Afternoon" is sung by Helen as she seduces Paris (not the other way around) in her front yard, singing a superbly idiomatic lyric ("my rockin' chair will fit yer and my cake was never richer") accompanied by undulating vibes, winds, and bass. "Lazy Afternoon" has been a cabaret staple for years, and the song was recorded by alt-rockers The Reivers in 1989 in what is a rocking but fairly respectful tribute version.

3.   "SMOKE GETS IN YOUR EYES" (FROM *ROBERTA*)

Jerome Kern and Otto Harbach's 1933 musical *Roberta* was a successful post-Princess Theatre musical about a college football star whose Aunt Minnie runs a dress shop in Paris (as the titular mam'selle Roberta). The show, based on the Alice Duer Miller novel, was star-studded, featuring an aging Fay Templeton, a young Bob Hope, Fred MacMurray, and George Murphy, and if Harbach's book was typically inane, Kern's score was not, for it gave us "Smoke Gets in Your Eyes."

The critic and historian Martin Gottfried has said

that the great composers can be rightly judged by the strength of their greatest song, and for Jerome Kern, that song is "Smoke Gets in Your Eyes." With Kern's tune wedded to one of the greatest lyrics ever written for an American popular song, "Smoke" was popular in the show and became more popular in the Fred Astaire-Ginger Rogers film version of *Roberta*. But most people must know this great song from the single cut by the Platters. Number One on the charts for three weeks in 1959, the Platters' version rescued a dormant title (a feat publicly acknowledged by no less a high priest than Oscar Hammerstein II) and made the song sing to future generations.

4. "MACK THE KNIFE" (FROM *THE THREEPENNY OPERA*)

One of the twentieth century's great works of theater, *The Threepenny Opera*, yielded one of the century's great melodies, Kurt Weill's A-minor "Moritat von Mackie Messer," with Bertolt Brecht's brilliant, cynical lyric translating as "The Moritat (ballad) of Mackie the Knife." *The Threepenny Opera* came and went quickly on Broadway in 1933, but the piece gained acceptance as a classic, particularly in Europe, and was revived off-Broadway in 1955 at the Theatre de Lys. Marc Blitz-stein's Eisenhower-era bowdlerization of *Threepenny* slowly became one of the biggest hits in off-Broadway history.

It was this Blitzstein translation that crooner Bobby Darin had worked into his nightclub act, and he laid it down on vinyl in 1959, with a swingin' band behind him, subverting and somewhat neutralizing the lyric about the robber-killer Macheath, a/k/a Mack the Knife. The public snapped it up despite the subtext of the song, and Darin's recording hit Number One on the charts and became *Billboard*'s number two song of the year.

The dichotomy of the two versions of the song was not lost on the creators of the 1994 movie *Quiz Show*. Robert Redford opened his film with folks rushing to get home to see the popular quiz shows of the day, accompanied by Darin's version, and ended with a grainy Kinescope of grotesque audience faces laughing, oblivious to the scandals, as singer Lyle Lovett's somber version of the "Moritat" played.

5.   "TILL THERE WAS YOU" (FROM *THE MUSIC MAN*)

Meredith Willson's 1958 musical was hailed as a classic almost from the beginning, but amidst all the trombones and Shipoopis, the tender second act ballad of realization, "Till There Was You," was somewhat lost. Again, we can thank the kids for bringing it into the national consciousness: After pop songstress Peggy Lee recorded her version in 1961, the Beatles recorded it in July 1963, apparently influenced by her non-sentimental version, and included it on *With The Beatles* (known as *Meet The Beatles* in the US).

The Fab Four had been carrying "Till There Was You" around with them for some time (at least as far back as their audition for Decca Records), and they gave it a new feel, with Spanish guitars and a beguine beat, ending on a most un-Willson-esque F major chord with a major seventh. This version is easily the most famous of all, and many first-time listeners are surprised to discover the song wasn't originally a Latin number at all.

6. "HERE'S THAT RAINY DAY" (FROM *CARNIVAL IN FLANDERS*)

Johnny Carson's favorite song comes from what is easily the most obscure musical on this list. *Carnival in Flanders*, based on the award-winning 1936 French film *La Kermesse Heroique*, was a six-performance bomb as chaotic as a Breughel painting and about as easy to decipher. Wouldn't *you* think Johnny Burke, Jimmy Van Heusen, and Preston Sturges were the right guys to pen a medieval tuner set in a small Flemish town? Anybody?

Carnival in Flanders nevertheless gave us "Here's That Rainy Day," another wistful ballad for a rough year, and wisely gave it to Dolores Gray, who defined Sexy Middle Age on Broadway during the Golden Era. The late, great Gray won her Tony for 1953's *Flanders*, the shortest-running show to ever net a performer a Tony, and "Here's that Rainy Day" entered the jazz band and torch song repertoire, while at the same time capturing the attention of a certain talk-show host from Nebraska.

7. "ONE NIGHT IN BANGKOK" (FROM *CHESS*)

Unless you count Dolly Parton's "I Will Always Love You," written for the 1982 film version of *The Best Little Whorehouse in Texas* and made world famous by Whitney Houston ten years later, "One Night in Bangkok" is the last hit song from a musical to make the top of the pop charts.

A catchy piece of '80s junk-pop from the '80s junk-pop musical *Chess* made famous by the Murray Head single, "Bangkok" was written by Tim Rice, Benny Andersson, and Bjorn Ujlvaeus. The pre-sold success of the song insured the high profile of the show.

8. "SEND IN THE CLOWNS" (FROM *A LITTLE NIGHT MUSIC*)

Stephen Sondheim's one and only hit song (by himself, that is—*West Side Story* and *Gypsy* have done him just fine, thank you) wasn't yet a smash when *A Little Night Music* won six Tony Awards in 1973. It took pop singer Judy Collins (and her musical director, Jonathan Tunick, also Sondheim's orchestrator) to make it truly famous.

On her 1975 hit album, *Judith*, Collins delivered a simple, piano-accompanied version of "Send in the Clowns," preserving the undercurrent of regret and sadness inherent in the song (while somewhat obscuring the nocturne setting of the piece). Collins's version won Sondheim the Grammy Award for "Song of the Year" for 1975, and gave the song an entry into the popular consciousness it never would have received through the superb but somewhat rarified *Night Music*.

9. "SEPTEMBER SONG" (FROM *KNICKERBOCKER HOLIDAY*)

As beautiful a song as "September Song" is, it's actually quite a manipulative little piece in context. *Knickerbocker Holiday* concerns the life and times of Pieter Stuyvesant, the aging governor of New Amsterdam, and the Kurt Weill-Maxwell Anderson song is sung to convince his nubile young intended, Tina, to consider his suit in marriage, peg-leg, eye patch and all, instead of the young troublemaker she really loves, and to do it now.

"September Song" was written for the actor Walter Huston, a craggy persona with no real singing voice and no real vocal range. Weill wrote a verse which was short-lined and a chorus which was limited as far as range, leaving Huston ample opportunity to "act" the song and put it over that way. This he did, and his studio recording of the song was a hit even after the show closed.

Huston did not re-create his role in the 1944 film version of *Knickerbocker Holiday* (just as well—it's a bit of a bomb), but the song was still put over well by Charles Coburn, furthering its popularity. But Huston is the performer most people associate with "September Song," and since he was not primarily a musical theater talent, most people don't realize the song comes from a musical, let alone one as little-known as *Knickerbocker Holiday*.

10. YOU'LL NEVER WALK ALONE" (FROM *CAROUSEL*)

Here's one for the sports fans out there. The theme song of the most successful team in the history of English football ("soccer" to us Yanks) has as its motto and theme song a 1945 show tune by Rodgers and Hammerstein. But Liverpool FC and *Carousel*'s Billy Bigelow have much in common.

As Billy lays dead in *Carousel*, Nettie Fowler sings "You'll Never Walk Alone" to his grieving widow, giving her the strength to carry on. In 1966, with English football at the top of the world (hosting and winning the World Cup), Liverpool Football Club was on top of the domestic game. The supporters of the club unofficially adopted the version of "Walk Alone" performed by Liverpool band Gerry and the Pacemakers, the lyric matching the life-and-death importance the English give their football. The song is played as the players take the pitch to this day, and the club crest boasts the words "May you never walk alone." Even Pink Floyd incorporated a version of it into their 1971 *Meddle* LP.

I Love a Film Cliché
Movie Musicals that
Made It to the Stage

W hat people in the theater seem loath to acknowledge is that the state of the Broadway musical is
almost as creatively bankrupt as the much-maligned
movie industry—which is why the majority of the below
listed titles are current. Here are a few examples of
stage musicals adapted from movies.

1. *SINGIN' IN THE RAIN*

The film that many consider the pinnacle of the movie
musical, it's a flawless, joyous celebration of movement. The hilarious script (by Betty Comden and
Adolph Green) deals with Hollywood's awkward steps
from silents to talkies as well as the need for quality
rainwear.

The 1985 stage version, however, upset the sleek
screenplay by dropping in unnecessary extra numbers
("Hub Bub," an extended "Wedding of the Painted
Dolls") and giving other characters extraneous and
often downright unpleasant dialogue. Modern dance pioneer Twyla Tharp directed and choreographed, but

the show had little effect on a real live stage, where even the water seemed extraneous.

2. *42ND STREET*

This great 1933 movie musical was a backstage fable to begin with, and even as re-authored by Michael Stewart for a 1980 audience, it was pure showbiz corn from the word go. The classic story—Girl Off Turnip Truck who Dances Like an Angel gets job understudying Temperamental Star with Rich Boyfriend, Girl gets Fired by Star, Star breaks Leg, Desperate Producer Hires Girl back, Girl becomes Star of Biggest Hit Ever—was played with a clear-eyed sense of Broadway as Wonderland.

Thanks to director-choreographer Gower Champion, the show strutted in high style, with tap, jazz, ballet, and good old hoofing all on view in a chorus dancer's dream. The Abominable Showman himself, David Merrick, had his last great hit producing *42nd Street*, and the death of Gower Champion on the show's opening day added to the legend of this long-running show.

3. *SATURDAY NIGHT FEVER*

The fine 1978 disco movie, the coming-of-age story of Tony Manero, a working-class mook who finds himself on the disco floor on Saturday nights, was fleshed out for the Broadway stage in 1999. The legendary Bee Gees tunes from the film were augmented with other songs from the movie's soundtrack album, plus other disco-riffic hits of the era.

The show was clearly an attempt at '70's nostalgia, and the attempt to shoehorn the songs into the book was clunky (and probably doomed to failure). The lack of John Travolta's star presence didn't help either—the show boasted no stars, although it created one in the monomial Orfeh.

4. ***SEVEN BRIDES FOR SEVEN BROTHERS***

One of the finest musicals ever conceived for film, this 1954 adaptation of the bucolic tale "The Sobbin' Women" featured glorious CinemaScope photography and two of the best musical numbers ever shot, "Lonesome Polecat" and the immortal "Barn Raising," with choreography by the estimable Michael Kidd.

Opening on Broadway in the summer 1982, it should have been obvious that no stage adaptation could ever match the peerless film version, and the well-cast but ultimately pointless stage version closed in less than a week. It has gone on to a better life in regional theaters.

5. ***THE LION KING***

Disney's phenomenally popular 1994 animated film was adapted by some old friends (film composers Elton John and Hans Zimmer, lyricist Tim Rice, and librettist Irene Mecchi) as well as many new hands. But the guiding hand belonged to director and costume designer Julie Taymor.

While the film of *The Lion King* is occasionally lovely and visually worthy of the veldt setting, the 1998 Broadway version became a vision of almost unparalleled beauty and creativity. Taymor and the other designers, scenic designer Richard Hudson, and lighting designer Donald Holder, met the cinematic challenges in brilliantly theatrical ways, making the stage show a tribal ritual unfolding as the storytellers enact the tale for us, the audience.

6. *FOOTLOOSE*

A *fin de siécle* affection for all things '80s and kitsch is the only explanation for this dumb year 2000 stage adaptation of the dumb quasi-movie musical hit from 1982. If you care, it's about a free-spirited kid who's just gotta dance, and who has the misfortune to move to a town where no one is allowed to dance. No compelling reason is given as to why jitterbugging is ixnayed, but Bad Preacher Daddy is involved. Let me guess: Since it's a *musical*, I bet everybody ends up cutting a big rug at the end. Yes, indeed.

7. *THE PRODUCERS*

A smash that made New York and the world giddy with smash-hit-itis, *The Producers* is the stage version of Mel Brooks's great 1968 film comedy. The changes made to the movie for its adaptation to the musical stage in 2001 are a model example of the genre.

Brooks (and his co-librettist, Thomas Meehan) wisely re-set the tale in 1959, the end of Broadway's Golden Age, to point up Max Bialystock's many previous failures (shows like *South Passaic* and *High Button Jews*, for example). The songs Brooks added to the show delineated the characters better than dialogue would have, but the real ace in the hole was Susan Stroman's no-holds-barred direction and choreography. Maxing out her budget, she created one outrageous gag after another, sometimes with the help of the design team (singing pigeons with Nazi armbands) and sometimes with just an outrageous flourish (a chorus girl twisting herself into a swastika at the end of "Springtime for Hitler.")

8. *THE UMBRELLAS OF CHERBOURG*

Jacques Demy's 1964 musical masterpiece *Les Parap-luies de Cherbourg* is as cinematic a musical as there's ever been; it's a superb application of French New Wave film techniques to the movie musical genre. Fifteen years later, it was seen on the stage in New York under its English-language title, *The Umbrellas of Cherbourg*.

The score for *Umbrellas* is all-sung, with much of Michel Legrand's and Demy's score featuring stand-alone songs and recurring musical motifs which pre-date the European pop-operas to come from the likes of Andrew Lloyd Webber and Boublil and Schonberg. New York's Public Theater hosted the show, which was staged by Andrei Serban, a director with a noted eye for gorgeous stage pictures. Sheldon Harnick and Charles Burr translated the piece and used its English title, and while many agreed it was good to look at, it couldn't compare to the riot of color and level of experimentation seen in the movie version.

9. *GIGI*

Gigi was the Best Picture Oscar winner for 1958, a beautifully stylized *bonbon* based on Colette's novel of Gay Paree. A Broadway musical version, offered up in 1973, looked good but offered no improvements on the classic film.

The wondrous Alfred Drake was along to sing the Maurice Chevalier role, and audiences predictably enjoyed watching him "Sank Hay-ven for leetle gaaals," but aside from Drake and attractive décor, audiences found little to savor. Perhaps the novel's premise, a girl basically being purchased by an older man, was not a socially acceptable topic for a musical by the 70s.

10. *MEET ME IN ST. LOUIS*

Here we go again. Like *Gigi*, *Meet Me in St. Louis* was an attempt to take a classic MGM film musical and adapt it to the stage. And like *Gigi*, once again, the result was less than satisfying. Maybe the film's director, Vincente Minnelli, would have made the difference.

Audiences again saw little need to plunk down big bucks to see a stage show of a film they could easily rent on video, even though the 1989 version looked great and moved well. The additions made to the simple story, like a Halloween Skeleton's Ball, didn't help either.

We Sail the Seas
10 Musicals Set on the Water

Tales of the sea often conjure up romantic images of hardy sailors and bloodthirsty pirates—images ideally suited to musical theater. Here are ten musicals that were all wet.

1. *SHOW BOAT*

The seminal American musical, adapted and produced in 1927, from Edna Ferber's grand novel. Flo Ziegfeld produced it, and a good thing too, because an ordinary-looking production of this show might have killed it.

Jerome Kern and Oscar Hammerstein II forever separated the musical from the operetta by letting the libretto and the songs cue the characters. As much about the Mississippi and, by extension, America as it was about the titular boat, the *Cotton Blossom*, *Show Boat* is without question the American theater's most important musical.

2. *THE FROGS*

A very loose adaptation of Aristophanes by Burt Shevelove, with songs by Stephen Sondheim, originally performed in the Yale University swimming pool in 1974. It's supposed to be a spectacle, but with two of the authors of *A Funny Thing Happened on the Way to the Forum* on hand, you never know just what kind of spectacle you've got. "The time is the present. The place is ancient Greece."

Dionysos is traveling to the underworld, but gets waylaid by Charon and some frogs while on the river Styx. Or something like that. Then Shakespeare and Shaw start debating the value of art in society. Or something like that. Sondheim squeezes in a gorgeous setting of Shakespeare's "Fear No More," and the actors don't need to shower before they leave.

3. *BILLY*

A rightly forgotten one-performance bomb, this 1969 rock musical took as its source Herman Melville's novel *Billy Budd*. Unfortunately, they played it for anti-war counterculture points instead of grasping the political and sexual allegory inherent in the Melville novel. Fortunately, no one cared. When people weren't looking at Ming Cho Lee's rope-ladder-playground ship set, they had to focus on the action. Too bad.

4. *ANYTHING GOES*

When the *Lusitania* sank, Cole Porter's idea of a shipwreck musical sank with it. Years later, he wrote a shipboard story instead, and *Anything Goes* was the result. Great songs and the presence of first-class talent elevated this typical 1930's screwball farce plot into a classic show.

Ethel Merman was Reno Sweeney, ship's entertainer and part-time evangelist (so Porter could write a faux-spiritual, "Blow, Gabriel, Blow") and William Gaxton and Victor Moore were the clowns. The *echt*-thirties plot involves rich socialites, wacky gangsters, and Chinese guys. It's more fun than it sounds.

5. *BIG RIVER*

The great American novel, Mark Twain's *The Adventures of Huckleberry Finn*, was adapted into a Broadway musical in time for the 1984–85 Broadway season, following a gestation period at American Repertory Theater and La Jolla Playhouse. La Jolla's Artistic Director, Des McAnuff, appealed to country songwriter Roger Miller to supply the score, and Miller's simple tunes and Spartan lyrics suited the show just fine.

Set largely on Huck and Jim's raft, the show won seven Tony Awards (including the first Scenic Design Tony awarded to a woman, for Heidi Landesman's brilliant evocation of the Mighty Mississippi; the river became almost a character itself) and ran for 1,005 performances on Broadway.

6. *DAMES AT SEA*

This ultra-spoofy 1968 off-Broadway musical hit was about, well, showbiz and boats. Bernadette Peters made her first big splash (ahem) in this homage to shipboard musicals, à la *Anything Goes*, and backstage musicals, à la *42nd Street*. A musical set on a ship has to perform on a ship for real after that nasty ol' Depression tears the theater down. Sweet chorus nobody Ruby (Keeler?) saves the day, with the help of her Uncle Sam.

7. *THE NEW MOON*

This delightful Broadway operetta from 1928 is perhaps the last of the great "Broadway operettas." Sigmund Romberg and Oscar Hammerstein II gave audiences one of the strongest scores in history, with hits like "Softly, As In a Morning Sunrise," "Lover, Come Back to Me," "Wanting You," and the classic march "Stouthearted Men." The typically grandiose plot concerns dashing French revolutionaries, beautiful maidens, and terror and heroism on the high seas, as the *New Moon* sails from France to the Louisiana territory.

8. *Sail Away*

Noel Coward's 1961 shipboard musical comedy starred the priceless Elaine Stritch as Miss Paragon, the put-upon cruise director aboard the S.S. *Coronia*. Stritch's part was built up in previews, when it was apparent that a darker subplot, involving an unhappy wife on a solo cruise, was not working. Coward did his usual all-me writing job and was greatly amused when critics attacked the piece for being paper thin and almost plotless, when Coward obviously had been writing fluff all along.

9. *Titanic*

A somewhat troubled show in previews, due to its technical requirements, this elegant setting of the doomed ocean liner's only voyage survived much tinkering to win the Tony for Best Musical in 1997 (and, FYI, it came out before the movie did).

Composer-lyricist Maury Yeston and librettist Peter Stone took characters from history (the Astors, ship's architect Andrews) and invented others drawn from history (crew members, three Irish girls named Kate). Yeston's music soared, particularly in the choral writing, and praise was unanimous for Stewart Laing's marvelous geometric sets, which tilted ominously as the evening went on.

10. *MUTINY!*

This middling British pop opera from 1985 was based on *Mutiny on the Bounty*. Written by English pop artist/actor David Essex and Richard Crane, and starring Essex, it played for a year and a half in London's West End. A truly spectacular set and good intentions notwithstanding, if a show has a song called "Breadfruit," *and* features an exclamation point in the title, *and* doesn't take place in Oklahoma, then you're asking for it.

I'm a Bad, Bad Man
10 Great Musical Villains

Most musicals are a fight between the forces of good and evil. Here are ten musical baddies, all wretched, all memorable, all juicy.

1. JUDGE TURPIN, SWEENEY TODD

One of the creepiest characters to ever grace a musical, *Sweeney Todd*'s Judge Turpin is a miserable, pious lech who ruins an entire family before meeting his bloody comeuppance. Turpin condemns barber Todd to prison in Australia and rapes his wife, driving her insane. Todd finally slits the Judge's throat as he sits in Todd's barber chair.

2. *THE PHANTOM OF THE OPERA*

Gaston Leroux's gothic villain is a hideously deformed creature living in the bowels of the Paris Opera House. Andrew Lloyd Webber's 1985 musical version, masterfully directed by Harold Prince, presents the Phantom, memorably portrayed by Michael Crawford in London and New York, in all his dark glory. Though physically repellent, The Phantom harbors a deep romantic passion for art and beauty. Driven by an obsessive love for opera ingenue Christine Daae, he extorts, murders, and kidnaps to feed his neurasthenic needs.

3. JUD FRY, *OKLAHOMA!*

With his physical unpleasantness, remote personality, and dank hideout, *Oklahoma!*'s Jud Fry is a sort of cousin to the Phantom. Jud, Aunt Eller's ranch hand, lives out back in the smokehouse. Also like the Phantom, he has his own obsession, this one with Eller's niece, Laurey. Not so much villainous as just plain creepy in the first act, his rage at losing Laurey to cowboy Curly turns truly dangerous in the second act, as he sets fire to a haystack during Curly and Laurey's wedding shivaree.

4. MISS HANNIGAN, *ANNIE*

She's often hung over, she smokes like a chimney, and she likes to spank her charges. Well, *Annie*'s Miss Hannigan certainly wins no points for Mother of the Year. And yet, in her greatest act of villainy, that's exactly what the lousy orphanage moll tries to do: Pass a friend off as orphan Annie's mother to get next to Daddy Warbucks and claim his fortune. Every actress, from Dorothy Loudon, Nell Carter, and June Havoc onstage, to Carol Burnett onscreen, and Kathy Bates on television, has gotten her Depression-era grasping for the good life on "Easy Street" just right.

5. MORDRED, *CAMELOT*

At least Mordred comes by his bitterness honestly: He's King Arthur's illegitimate son. (That must look awful on a resume.) As soon as he's an adult, or what passed for an adult in the days of Lerner and Loewe's 1960 musical *Camelot*, he declares "Fie on Goodness" and proceeds to take up arms in protest of his father's moral code. Purely distilled by Alan Jay Lerner from Mallory and T.H. White, he's easily interpreted as the Nazi element threatening Arthur's democracy.

6.   BILL SIKES, *OLIVER!*

Bill Sikes is a typically Dickensian villain, and he's given appropriately rude and crude music to establish him in Lionel Bart's colorful score for *Oliver!* Bart disobeyed many of the American ground rules for musical writing, and simply had the murderous Sikes thunder on, stand in a doorway, and tell everyone how awful he is. We see just how awful at show's end when he murders his Nancy.

7.   GENERAL BULLMOOSE, *LI'L ABNER*

The *Li'l Abner* comics were full of colorful characters blown up from reality. General Bullmoose was creator Al Capp's ruthless capitalist, an Eisenhower-era baddie derived from Ike's Secretary of Defense, Charles E. Wilson ("What's good for General Motors is good for the country"). Bullmoose (about whom is sung, "What's good for General Bullmoose/Is good for the U.S.A!") wants to corner the market on Yokumberry tonic and is prepared to kill Li'l Abner to do so, but he's hyp-mo-tized by Evil Eye Fleegle into admitting the truth. A typically satirical end for this Cappian creation.

8.   SEN. BILLBOARD RAWKINS, *FINIAN'S RAINBOW*

Not too far from Bullmoose on the demagogue scale, Sen. Billboard Rawkins was a caricature of reconstructionist Senators Bilbo and Rankin. In *Finian's Rainbow*, he's a buffoon who wants to evict the honest share-croppers of Rainbow Valley from their land in order to profit from the wonders of uranium. He's turned black (oh, great) by a wish on an enchanted crock of gold, and after walking a mile (and dancing "The Begat") in the sharecroppers' shoes, he repents and spreads goodwill to the folks of the Valley.

9.   INSPECTOR JAVERT, LES MISÉRABLES

A special sub-category of villain, the principled villain, is headed by *Les Misérables*' Inspector Javert. In every incarnation of Hugo's epic tale, Javert is a single-minded nemesis to the hero, Jean Valjean. As Valjean seeks to put his past life of petty crime behind him, Javert stays on his trail, doggedly pursuing his elusive prey regardless of circumstance. "My duty's to the law, you have no rights," he sings as he first corners Valjean, in the 1985 musical smash. When, near the end of the musical, Valjean saves Javert's life and escapes again, Javert, unable to cope with the perversions of justice and logic, takes his own life.

10.   EVE HARRINGTON, *APPLAUSE*

"Eve! You four-star bitch! Thank you!" So cries Margo Channing at the conclusion of *Applause*, the 1970 musical version of the legendary story and film *All About Eve*. Eve Harrington is a schemer, plain and simple, determined to become a famous actress at any cost. She wins the trust of her heroine, Margo, then proceeds to win almost everything else in Margo's life, ruthlessly climbing the ladder of success all the way to the Tony Awards, where Margo, prodded out of complacency by Eve's scheming, finally realizes that her most prized possession is the love and trust of her man.

Blow, Gabriel, Blow
Depictions of Faith in Broadway Musicals

I t is a topic as elemental as existence itself. It is one of the main subjects in the American consciousness. It's religious faith, and many long to see honest depictions of faith and religion on the musical stage. Here are ten musicals that vary in their attitudes toward faith, but present an honest witness.

1. *THE GOSPEL AT COLONUS*

Avant-garde theater artist Lee Breuer came about as close to a mainstream Broadway musical as he ever will with this 1988 Broadway effort with music by Bob Telson. Breuer's idea was a setting of Sophocles's *Oedipus at Colonus* as told by a Pentecostal Sunday service, a melding of the Christian faith and the Greek *catharsis*. *The Gospel at Colonus* premiered at the Brooklyn Academy of Music's Next Wave Festival in 1983.

As presided over by the magisterial Morgan Freeman, the evening was praised in concept but left most reviewers scratching their heads to comprehend the meaning. The main pleasures, besides Freeman, were Telson's music, the predictably fine Gospel singers (massed choirs and soloists), and Alison Yerxa's impressive church altar set.

2. LOST IN THE STARS

Adapted from Alan Paton's novel *Cry, the Beloved Country*, Kurt Weill and Maxwell Anderson's 1949 musical *Lost in the Stars* was Weill's last musical and a searing examination of faith in crisis and hope for change fueled by racial injustice. Reverend Stephen Kumalo, whose son, Absalom, is missing, journeys from his home in the South African hills to the shantytowns and city streets of Johannesburg to find him, fearing that Absalom has lost his way, both spiritually and physically. The show as a whole was appreciated but not raved over, but the score served Paton's minimalist prose well, particularly in the haunting "Train to Johannesburg" and the title song, in which Reverend Kumalo questions his faith in an absentee God.

3. *JOSEPH AND THE AMAZING TECHNICOLOR DREAMCOAT*

The most profitable kids' pageant ever conceived, Tim Rice and Andrew Lloyd Webber's *Joseph and the Amazing Technicolor Dreamcoat* was indeed written to be performed by and for the kids at Colet Court, the prep school for London's St. Paul's. (It was a commission from the school's choirmaster, who was a Webber family friend.) Their tale was the tale of Joseph, the dreamer and coat-wearer, from the book of Genesis.

The anything-goes pop ethos of the late sixties, coupled with the audience for whom they were writing, gave Rice and Lloyd Webber freedom to mix styles and genres freely in the piece, and after its premiere in May 1968, it kept growing. Jacob's favorite son finally made it to Broadway in 1981 and has proven a huge cash cow both occasionally on the Main Stem, and especially on the road.

4. CABIN IN THE SKY

Vernon Duke and John Latouche wrote the remarkable score to this adaptation (by Lynn Root) of the folk play *The Green Pastures* by Marc Connelly. Its premiere in 1940 was an important event, not just because of its intelligent and human black characters, but because of its attitude towards faith and spirituality.

Cabin in the Sky takes the form of a parable in Negro dialect: The Lawd's General and Lucifer, Jr. are fighting for the soul of Little Joe, a decent Everyman given to earthly temptations (here, notably gambling and Miss Georgia Brown, Junior's emissary of hotcha). Joe's wife, Petunia (Ethel Waters, in her only Broadway musical), fights the good fight to keep him on the straight and narrow, and her outlook and her unwavering goodness is what gives *Cabin in the Sky* its appeal. Indeed, the "Cabin" she sings of is not only Heaven, but also the perfect life in faith and love on Earth.

5. LES MISÉRABLES

Much has been written about the mega-smash musical *Les Misérables* and its tribute to the power of the human spirit. But Victor Hugo's classic novel, on which the musical is faithfully based, offers a stirring look at the faith that carried France through much of the eighteenth and nineteenth centuries.

The hero of *Les Miz*, Jean Valjean, looks to God at

almost every turn and is saved from returning to prison and ruining his life again by the Bishop of Digne, who not only spares Valjean from prison, but also gifts him candlesticks with which Valjean starts his life anew. He is, of course, pursued at every turn by the show's principled villain, Inspector Javert. Both Javert and Valjean are given fervent anthems of faith and guidance, Javert's "Stars" his declaration of determination, and Valjean's "Bring Him Home" a prayer for delivery on the eve of battle.

6. **LEONARD BERNSTEIN'S *MASS***

Leonard Bernstein wore many, many hats in his rich life, and two of them were Professional Jew and Friend of President John F. Kennedy. His friendship with the Catholic First Family fueled his fascination with Roman Catholicism, and when he was asked to commemorate the opening of Washington's Kennedy Center in 1970, he decided to honor the late President with a unique modern Mass.

A synthesis of the Latin texts of the Catholic Mass, presided over by a celebrant, and modern commentary on the state of belief and faith as they provided by singing and dancing characters, *Mass* was a mammoth spectacle, employing two orchestras, a marching band, a choir, a children's choir, dancers, soloists, and the head of Alfredo Garcia. Packed inside the spectacle were the usual Bernstein musical and textual indulgences (many with subpar lyrics by Stephen Schwartz), such as a Gospel sermon in 7/8 time, and the "touch of peace" concluding the ceremony. But also present was some perfectly sublime music, including the plaintive "Thank You," and one of the finest American songs ever written, "A Simple Song."

7. *FIDDLER ON THE ROOF*

Sholom Aleichem's stories, particularly "Tevye and his Daughters," are rich in folk wisdom and humor and especially strong faith and belief. This pure belief is what keeps simple dairyman Tevye going and is also what attracted Zero Mostel to the character and to *Fiddler on the Roof* in the first place.

Tevye's man-to-Man conversations with God are a gently humorous device to illustrate Tevye's beliefs, but the show's musical moments are even richer in spirituality. Tevye's "want" song, "If I Were a Rich Man," starts as one of those conversations, and the musical high point of the evening is the unimpeachable, so-simple-it-hurts "Sabbath Prayer."

8. *BRIGADOON*

Lerner and Loewe's magical musical sets up two very different schools of belief. Brigadoon, the village which appears only one day every hundred years, was saved from pagan witches by the sacrifice of Mr. Forsythe, a "minister of the kirk," who was basically a benevolent totalitarian. Invading this world is the outsider, Tommy Albright, an Amerian with postwar malaise, who desperately needs something to believe in.

Not much is spoken of theocratic religion in *Brigadoon*, but the basic theme of redemption through faith is powerfully present, especially in the "From This Day On," the heartbreaking duet between Tommy and Fiona, the village lass with whom he's fallen unconditionally in love, and he must give up in order to get back.

9. *FALSETTOLAND*

William Finn and James Lapine's nervy trilogy, the "Marvin Songs," followed Marvin, an immature, con-

flicted husband and father who left his family for another man. Episode three, *Falsettoland*, set in 1981,
examines the extended family dynamics set up by the
consequences of these actions: Marvin's lover, Whizzer, is diagnosed with what turns out to be AIDS, and
Marvin's son, Jason, is approaching his bar mitzvah.

The analogy is fairly routine: Jason's passage into
manhood through the Jewish bar mitzvah ritual plaes
in comparison to the life lesson the death of his father's
lover will teach him. But so deep is Jason's belief in the
power of love that his ideas of "the miracle of Judaism"
change over the course of the show, from picking
which girls he'll invite to the ceremony to holding the
ritual in Whizzer's hospital room, in the hopes that he
won't die.

10. *Man of La Mancha*

Joe Darion and Mitch Leigh's 1965 musical *Man of La
Mancha* is adapted from Cervantes's classic novel *Don
Quixote*, the story of a knight–errant and his doomed
quest for truth and beauty. As dramatized, Cervantes
himself is on trial and must defend his manuscript in
the kangaroo court of convicts judging him.

The youth-quake mid-sixties attitude was less
about chastity, purity, and devotion than it was about
success against odds and rebellion against authority.
But *Man of La Mancha* had belief in both sets of values,
the religious hypocrisy of the show's venal Padre and
Quixote's hollow-pious family offset by Quixote's unwavering faith in the abilities God has given him and his
redemptive power over his Dulcinea, the kitchen wench
Aldonza.

It's Better with a Bard

10 Musicals Based on Shakespeare

Foolhardy to adapt the works of the immortal Bard of Avon to the musical stage? Tosh and forsooth! These ten shows stepped bravely into the breach.

1. *WEST SIDE STORY*

This classic musical from 1957 updated *Romeo and Juliet.* Street gangs, native white and Puerto Rican immigrant—stand in for the Capulets and Montagues, and native boy and immigrant girl fell in love with tragic consequences. Arthur Laurents' book trimly handled the transition, inventing a kind of contempo slang for his gang kids, rife with "cracko jacko's" and "kid-dando's."

The parallels to Shakespeare matter less than the structure of the show, which moved in a way that no musical ever had. Jerome Robbins directed and choreographed the show to dance almost constantly, to the brilliant rhythms of Leonard Bernstein's eternal dance score. The movement of the gangs was Robbins' own heightened, stylized realism, which both underscored the tragedy and drove the action.

2. *YOUR OWN THING*

A radical change in attitude from (and towards) youth in 1968 was key in the creation of this musical version of *Twelfth Night*. The gender politics and examination of unconditional love that mark Shakespeare's play are spun cleverly in *Your Own Thing*, which makes no bones about Illyria-on-the-Hudson and the desires of the longhaired cast to do "their own thing" with long-haired man (or woman).

John Driver's very funny book used slides, cartoon thought balloons, and other then-new multimedia to comment on the Shakespeare (Viola: "Who governs here?" Mayor John V. Lindsay: "New York is a fun city." Cough, cough.), while jettisoning the clowns, letting a rock band, The Apocalypse, make the funny instead. A big hit off-Broadway, *Your Own Thing* is one of the most satisfying uses of Shakespeare in a musical context.

3. *THE BOYS FROM SYRACUSE*

George Abbott authored and directed this breezy 1938 farce based on *The Comedy of Errors*. The twins plot was maintained, and the part of the courtesan, who shows up to throw a wrench in the plans of her "Master Antipholus," was expanded for good, sexy comedy. But best of all was the score, one of the Rodgers and Hart classics. "The Shortest Day of the Year," "This Can't Be Love," and the riotous "Oh! Diogenes!" all point up the farce. A seriously rewritten version was presented, to little acclaim, on Broadway in 2002.

4. SHAKESPEARE'S CABARET

Talented composer Lance Mulcahy conceived this intriguing evening, setting many of the Bard's words to
music. Developed off-Broadway at the Colonnades
Lab, Mulcahy's pen embraced Shakespearean verse
both familiar ("Shall I Compare Thee to a Summer's
Day?," "If Music Be the Food of Love") and less so
("Crabbed Age and Youth," from *The Passionate Pil-
grim*). Despite the show's lasting only fifty-four performances on Broadway in 1981, Mulcahy's music
received a Tony nomination.

5. TWO GENTLEMEN OF VERONA

Director Mel Shapiro asked Galt MacDermot to set
"Who is Silvia?" to music for his 1971 New York Shakespeare Festival production of *The Two Gentlemen of
Verona*. Shortly afterward, their "grand new musical"
version was the hit of the summer and moved on to win
the Best Musical Tony on Broadway later that season.

This musical version (which dropped "The" from
the Shakespeare) was a quite agreeable mix of musical
styles, with rock, soul, Latin, and even country jostling
for position. Shapiro's typically anachronistic direction
gave us a bustling Milan (and, thanks to wordsmith
John Guare, a pregnant Julia) which bore a striking resemblance to a scaffold-clad Manhattan. The youthful
tone of the show was served by a superb cast, including
Raul Julia and Clifton Davis as the two gents, with
Diana Davila and the luminous Jonelle Allen as their
ladies fair.

6. RETURN TO THE FORBIDDEN PLANET

This musical version of *The Tempest* was, pun intended, a monster hit in London but less so on Ameri-

can shores. The show's creator, Bob Carlton, had wanted to fashion a campy Shakespeare musical as a late-night offering on the London fringe, and word-of-mouth spread on *Return to the Forbidden Planet* like wildfire.

Planet was a major award winner after it opened in London in 1989 and remains a favorite on tour in the UK. The show's tacky approach to the rock tunes it incorporates may have doomed it in America. Weaving the *Tempest* plot points in with its '50s and '60s tunes and framing it all inside a *Forbidden Planet*-like cheeseball space flick (the film is based on *The Tempest*), this one practically screams "cult musical."

7. *KISS ME, KATE*

The great Cole Porter's greatest score brilliantly supports Sam and Bella Spewack's 1948 treatment of *The Taming of the Shrew*, which turns out to be a thorny rose to the theater biz (and, oh yes, a masterpiece of musical comedy). Smart, funny, tuneful– let's eat!

The Spewacks wrapped a musicalized *Shrew* around the onstage and offstage foibles of the troupe performing the show, trying it out on the road, in the "land of Mencken and Nod." Here's the egomaniacal director/star, his estranged wife, the star-crossed secondary couple, funny gangsters, and some of the very best songs ever written for the theater. Porter's beguine, "Were Thine That Special Face," is here, as is the minor-key scorcher, "Too Darn Hot," the torch song, "Why Can't You Behave?," and the funniest song ever written, "Brush Up Your Shakespeare." Check, please.

8. *ROCKABYE HAMLET*

A 1978 flop, *Rockabye Hamlet* is folly made flesh: Let's musicalize the greatest play in Western history! And make it a rock musical! That's really a concert! Here's the downside, though: It'll suck. (Cast member Meat Loaf called it "the most horrifying experience of my life.")

Hello, Dolly! director Gower Champion was a little at sea with this rock setting of *Hamlet*, the brainchild of Canadian Clifford Jones. Too much pumped-up, concert-style bombast couldn't hide the serious shortcomings of the amateurish score, which had songs called "Pass the Biscuits, Mama," "The Rosencrantz and Guildenstern Boogie," and Ros and Guil's set-up for Hamlet, "Have I Got a Girl For You." Stephen Sondheim, who makes pancakes better than *Rockabye Hamlet*, might have sued over that last one, if he gave a damn.

9. *THE DONKEY SHOW*

Another post-modern update of Shakespeare, this one takes *A Midsummer Night's Dream* and sets it in the glam world of New York disco clubs. It opened in 1999 and has proven tremendously popular.

Subtitled *A Midsummer Night's Disco*, *The Donkey Show* (so named because of Bottom's transformation) concerns club owner Oberon and his Puckish sidekick, Dr. Wheelgood, who feed four nightclub patrons a potion to set their emotions in motion. Spectators can join the company in shaking it on the dance floor or watch from the rafters.

10. *MUSIC IS*

Perhaps it's the cross-dressing, perhaps it's the exotic locale, perhaps it's those most musically apropos opening lines, but *Twelfth Night* has spawned numerous high-profile musical adaptations, including Broadway's *Play On!* in 1997, which moved the action to a swingin' Harlem and used Duke Ellington songs, and *Love and Let Love*, which around the same time of the previously mentioned *Your Own Thing*, but fared much worse. Two thousand two brought *Illyria*, by Peter Mills, to New York.

Which brings us to 1976 and *Music Is*. Legendary showmeister George Abbott authored the book, with lyrics by Will Holt and music by the great Richard Adler (a longtime Abbott collaborator, dating back to *Damn Yankees* and *The Pajama Game*). Adler's work was probably the best thing about this unimaginative, straightforward treatment of *Twelfth Night*.

You're Responsible! You're the One to Blame! It's Your Fault!

10 Musicals to Scratch Your Head Over

S ome musicals can seem almost impossible for one reason or another, yet they end up being wonderful. But some ideas for musicals are just so hard to believe that to learn of their very existence is to smack one's forehead. Here are ten musicals whose existence remains, as the King of Siam said, a puzzlement.

1. *INTO THE LIGHT*

Perhaps the all-time head-scratcher, this six-performance 1986 bomb was the work of folks who decided there was something Broadway-worthy in the Holy Shroud of Turin. All serious questions of faith aside, how does one make scientists and religious figures look credible when they have to sing and dance? And since the shroud's veracity is still an open question, what's the point?

2. *BRING BACK BIRDIE*

This 1981 horror is People's Exhibit A as to why sequels never work in musicals. The great *Bye Bye Birdie*
told its tale and went its way, and there was no pressing
need to pick up with these characters twenty years
later. Especially not when Birdie is an overweight Elvis
clone, teen couple Kim and Hugo are nowhere in sight,
and Rosie and Albert's kids are in a punk rock band.
But a smash is a smash, and many felt the desire to
update the tale, suggesting that economics really ruled
the day. Four performances later, everyone felt much,
much dumber.

3. *A DOLL'S LIFE*

Another ill-advised catch-up job, *A Doll's Life* examined what happened after Nora Helmer slammed the
door and walked out of her husband Torvald's life in
Ibsen's *A Doll's House*. Why, exactly? Add to this the
conceit of having the actors playing these roles in rehearsal for a production of the Ibsen play, only to warp
into the musical's reality, and the head-scratching in-
creases. Despite the presence of old pros Harold
Prince, Larry Grossman, Betty Comden, and Adolph
Green, 1982's *A Doll's Life* never made much theatrical
sense.

4. *RACHAEL LILY ROSENBLOOM (AND DON'T YOU EVER FORGET IT!)*

A show with a defiantly gay-camp point of view, *Rachael Lily Rosenbloom* (the extra "A" in "Rachael"
being the one Barbra Streisand dropped) told the rags-
to-bitches story of the eponymous heroine, from kitten-
ish maid to ferocious movie star. Tom Eyen (who later

mainstreamed this story into *Dreamgirls*) and Paul Ja-
bara wrote it, and a weird, in-no-way-coked-out-of-
everyone's-mind time was had by all. Until it closed
after a week of previews.

5.   *ONE NIGHT STAND*

The great Jule Styne (*Gypsy, Bells are Ringing*) collaborated with playwright Herb Gardner (*I'm Not Rap-
paport, A Thousand Clowns*) on this 1980 eye-blinker
about a tunesmith who intends to kill himself for our
entertainment. The show proper was the back-story to
the aforementioned suicide, but why anyone ever
thought it should have been a musical is a question for
the ages. It closed during its tryout period en route to
Broadway.

6.   *GONE WITH THE WIND*

Yes, indeed. The grandest, most spectacular tale ever
told on film was given the musical treatment in 1973,
and to the surprise of many, it wasn't laughed out of
the country. Actually, it *started* out of the country, in
Japan in 1970, as *Scarlett*, with a score by the estimable Harold Rome and staging by Joe Layton. Playwright
Horton Foote came aboard for the pre-Broadway tryout, when the name changed to *GWTW*, starring Les-
ley-Ann Warren and Pernell Roberts. The show closed
on the road to Broadway after the critics weighed in
with predictable pans. While much of the show was intriguing, just why they bothered to try making it a
Broadway musical is still a mystery.

7.   *BEATLEMANIA*

Well, at least this one was kind of a hit. *Beatlemania*
was, basically, a cover band. Basically just four guys

who may or may not have looked and/or sounded like the Beatles, playing instruments and wearing a huge variety of time-specific costumes and wigs in front of time-specific "1960s" projections. Listen up, everybody, four guys up on stage dressed in Sgt. Pepper outfits *doesn't make them the Beatles*. And it ran for 920 performances! And then they made a movie out of it! What the hell is wrong with us?

8. *WELCOME TO THE CLUB*

There seem to be two Cy Colemans: Classy Cy, who writes *City of Angels*, *Sweet Charity*, and other sleek shows, and Tacky Cy, who indulges his trashy impulses and puts them onstage. Results include *I Love My Wife* ('70s swingers), *The Life* (hookers and pimps in Times Square), and the least successful of these shows, 1989's *Welcome to the Club*.

Welcome to the Club concerns a bunch of stereotypes in alimony jail, with only their thoughts to bail them out. Seemingly as stuck in the '70s as the other two Tacky Cy shows, its leering, Leroy Lockhorn–style take on women and relationships was well out of place in 1989, not to mention cheaply produced.

9. *THE CIVIL WAR*

Composer/lyricist Frank Wildhorn had some success with two late-1990s musicals, *Jekyll & Hyde* in 1997 and *The Scarlet Pimpernel* in 1998. Both these shows featured power-pop scores rather well suited to their "Classics Illustrated" sources, and enough fan interest to make their progress at least interesting. His next Broadway show, 1999's *The Civil War*, was more, and ultimately less, of the same. *The Civil War*, with lyrics by Jack Murphy, began as a double pop-album project, with Wildhorn's pop-soup ballads and pastiche rousers recorded by the likes of Hootie and the Blowfish and Travis Tritt. While the recording again stirred some interest, the lack of a linear story line to hang these songs on (the book was cobbled together from letters and speeches of the period) should have been evidence enough that it wouldn't work onstage, and indeed it didn't. Critics and audiences dismissed the show as eminently unworthy of its subject matter.

10. *DANCE OF THE VAMPIRES*

Yet another show ill suited to Broadway, 2002's *Dance of the Vampires* (adapted from the movie *The Fearless Vampire Killers*) is a piece of Euro-trash retro fitted for a camp audience in New York. To New York's credit, it didn't take. At all.

Adapted from the Viennese pop-opera smash *Tanz der Vampire*, songwriter Jim Steinman collaborated with playwright David Ives and original author Michael Kunze on the new version. *Vampires* is set in, oh dear, Lower Belabartokovitch and concerns the restless Count von Krolock, locked in a good-and-evil struggle for the soul of . . . someone to bite, maybe?

Peppered with lines like "God has left the building," the new book obviously aimed for good campy fun, but the score was not suitably altered to match the book, and it showed. *Vampire* never would have risked Broadway were it not for the presence of its star, Michael Crawford, whose magnetic performance in *The Phantom of the Opera* went a long way toward obscuring that show's goth-camp flaws.

Wig in a Box
10 Musicals Featuring Characters in Drag

S ince the dawn of theater, a man dressed as a lady (and, later, vice versa) has been a great way to get a laugh, and it's no different in musicals. Often, however, musical theater writers have used drag characters and situations for something more substantial.

1. *WHERE'S CHARLEY?*

1948 brought *Where's Charley?* to Broadway. *Charley*, featuring Frank Loesser's first Broadway score, was adapted by George Abbott from Brandon Thomas's 1892 farce *Charley's Aunt*. The type of play for which the term "warhorse" was invented, it involves forbidden romance, spinsters, lovestruck youth, and mistaken identity. And a man in drag.

Legendary clown Ray Bolger played lovesick Charley Wykeham, who dresses as his own spinster aunt to gain access to his beloved Amy Spettigue (played by the lovely Allyn Ann McLerie). Madcap hilarity ensues. Bolger took the show's hit, "Once in Love with Amy," and turned the gentle stroll into an audience sing-along number which endeared him further to the crowds, helping to turn the charming show into a 792-performance hit.

2. *A FUNNY THING HAPPENED ON THE WAY TO THE FORUM*

The plays of Plautus were the basis for this supreme farce, in which the drag doesn't occur until late in the second act. The musical's authors, Stepehen Sondheim, Larry Gelbart, and Burt Shevelove, made sure that the inevitable cross-dressing propelled the action, rather than distracted from it.

Pseudolus, a slave who will do anything to win his freedom, has enlisted the help of the ninny slave Hysterium, who must dress as a warrior's deceased virgin bride-to-be in order to fool him, while Pseudolus spirits said virgin away, very much alive, to his master, Hero. (Trust me, it's funnier than it sounds.) Since every character in this farce is a type (henpecked husband, wizened old man, vainglorious soldier, etc.), all eyes are fooled when Hysterium appears, scored to an ironic reprise of the ballad "Lovely," as the golden-haired angel. The show reaches its acme in the mad chase that ensues.

3. *LA CAGE AUX FOLLES*

A drag musical with a point of view, 1983's *La Cage aux Folles* takes its inspiration from the French farce of the same name. The main characters are the owner of a drag club on the French Riviera and his lover, the club's star attraction. The plot is set in motion by the impending marriage of the club owner's son.

The owner, Georges, and his lover, Albin, are living a fairly domestic life (so Harvey Fierstein's libretto tells us), until they learn that Michel, Georges' son from a one-night assignation, is engaged to the daughter of a notoriously conservative politician. Jerry Herman's score (his last for Broadway to date) delineates each lead: Georges, solid and masculine, and Albin, defiantly effeminate. Albin's anthem of self-assuredness, "I Am What I Am," ends the first act, as he doffs his wig before storming off stage.

This move backfires later, as Albin, in drag as Michel's "mother," doffs his wig by mistake at another nightclub, to the horror of the conservative couple. Finally, to slip past the press, the politician must dress in drag himself. "Honor thy father and mother," Fierstein stated, was the theme of this smash hit, and though the journey is unusual, the end result is indeed, worthy of the term "family values."

4. *THE MYSTERY OF EDWIN DROOD*

Rupert Holmes, pop recording artist, picked up a copy of Charles Dickens' unfinished novel *The Mystery of Edwin Drood* prior to a train trip, and by the end of his journey, he knew he wanted to make a musical out of it. The trouble inherent in musicalizing the moody tale of a young dandy, his troubled uncle, and the woman who comes between them was simple: It wasn't finished.

Holmes had his project adopted by Joseph Papp's Public Theater in New York, who presented it in Central Park in the summer of 1985, prior to bringing it to Broadway for a Tony-winning run. Holmes wrote the book, music, lyrics, and the orchestrations, a nearly-unprecedented quadruple.

The task of finishing Dickens's tale was assigned to the audience, who voted a different detective, murderer, and set of lovers each night, and the whole show was placed within the context of a "performance" of *Drood* by the Music Hall Royale. As befits a music-hall setting, one of the leads was a "pants" role, a man's part (Edwin Drood) played by "Miss Alice Nutting," the diva of the Royale.

5. *THE PRODUCERS*

Broadway received a much-needed shot in the arm with the appearance of *The Producers* in the spring of 2001. Hitting the Main Stem with almost-unprecedented anticipatory hoopla, it surpassed all expectations. Not bad for a show with something to offend everybody.

Mel Brooks' 1968 movie *The Producers* is a slapdash but often riotously funny farce about a theater producer (Zero Mostel) who takes on a nebbishy partner (Gene Wilder) by convincing him they can make more profit off a flop than a hit show. They proceed to find the worst possible play and hire the worst possible director, Roger DeBris, and the result is the jaw-dropping *Springtime for Hitler*. And of course, it becomes the hit of the season, leaving the two producers to ponder where they went right.

It seems more of an insult to Hitler nowadays to have him played by DeBris, a screaming drag queen, than by an innocent hippie, as he was in the film. As portrayed originally by Gary Beach, DeBris (assisted by his confidante, Carmen Ghia) enters in a gown resembling New York City's Chrysler Building and gets more outrageous from there. The drag quotient is upped in the first-act finale, as the stage fills with little old ladies, the pigeons Lane has been "plucking" to finance his show. The ladies *and* gentlemen of the ensemble totter on, dressed as old biddies, clicking their walkers in unison and singing of the joys of geriatric sex.

6. *HEDWIG AND THE ANGRY INCH*

Hedwig and the Angry Inch is the 1998 brainchild of John Cameron Mitchell, an appealing singing actor who penned this musical saga (with music by Stephen Trask) about a German "girly-boy" named Hedwig, whose failed sex-change operation results in the aforementioned "angry inch."

Hedwig's tale is one of unrequited love for an American GI who used and abused him before becoming the rock star Hedwig always wanted to be. Hedwig hits the road with his own band, called the Angry Inch, and stalks his beloved from afar. Hedwig is played by a man in fearless and fantastic drag (Mitchell wrote himself literally dozens of costume changes), and Trask and Mitchell's songs (aided off-Broadway by Trask's band, Cheater) tear into Hedwig's glam-rock dream world.

7. *SUGAR*

This is the musical version of the great film *Some Like it Hot*, wherein two struggling Chicago musicians witness the St. Valentine's Day Massacre and are forced to take it on the lam. Lambs they ain't but gams they got, as our heroes join an all-girl band bound for Florida.

Following the formula and story of the film, our boys pile double entendres upon cheap jokes as they're forced to swish around, evading the gangsters and the amorous attentions of Osgood the millionaire and Sugar the bombshell. *Sugar* was producer David Merrick's "big show" for 1972. Gower Champion briskly staged the capers, and Jule Styne and Bob Merrill's score kept Peter Brook's script moving along. But despite some success, the musical suffers in comparison to the great movie version, the greatest drag comedy ever.

8. *THE ROCKY HORROR SHOW*

Most anyone who buys this book is aware of the audience shenanigans that accompany a showing of *The Rocky Horror Picture Show*, a minor movie musical which gained legendary status thanks to midnight showings attended by diehard fans. The fans create their own show, hurling toast, rice, and their own dialogue at the screen and showing up in costume as their favorite characters.

But before there was the film, there was the stage musical. *The Rocky Horror Show* began as a fringe entertainment in England in 1973, making it to Broadway in 1975. The show is a mile-high-camp spoof of schlock horror movies and '50s drive-in specials as innocent Janet and Brad spend a dark and stormy night in the mansion of Dr. Frank-N-Furter. Furter is a drag nightmare, in outrageous makeup and ladies' lingerie, and he proceeds to turn the square couple on, over, and inside out.

Broadway saw *Rocky Horror* again in 2001, after icon status had been bestowed on the property, and the drag was as flamboyant as ever, yet seemed as comfortable as a pair of old shoes doing the "Time Warp."

9. *PAGEANT*

Drag musicals reached a kind of apotheosis with this 1991 off-off-Broadway evening, conceived by its director, Robert Longbottom. The work of Frank Kelly, Albert Evans, and Bill Russell, *Pageant* was literally a beauty pageant, with the performers (named Miss Bible Belt, Miss Industrial Northwest, and the like) played by men. Hosted by an unctuous emcee, *Pageant* was more clever than funny, though it had mild success in regional theater.

10. *THE BALLAD OF LITTLE JO*

Based on a true story and a 1993 movie of the same name, Mike Reid and Sarah Schlesinger's The *Ballad of Little Jo* had its premiere at Chicago's vaunted Steppenwolf Theater Company in 2000. More than a drag show, *Little Jo* is an examination of the roles expected of men and women on the Western frontier in the wake of the Civil War.

Josephine Monaghan, ostracized by her family for bearing a child out of wedlock, lands in Silver City, Idaho, and dons men's clothes, passing as a man to survive on her own. She falls in love with both her business partner *and* the man's wife, enacting a sort of *Twelfth Night*-on-the-range. Judy Kuhn's touching performance as Jo went a long way towards balancing out irregularities in the storytelling and the pleasant, but contrived, score.

Bigger Isn't Better
10 "Small" Shows

Although the big, splashy musicals normally bring in the big crowds, and therefore the big bucks, smaller musicals have sprung up by necessity; not everyone can afford big-ticket musicals, and many prefer a more intimate style of musical theater. These ten small musicals have been seen all over, Broadway and beyond.

1. *THE FANTASTICKS*

The prototypical small musical, with just two instruments—piano and harp—supporting a cast of nine. Tom Jones and Harvey Schmidt made their careers on this all-time long-running champion, which ran for over forty years at New York's tiny Sullivan Street Playhouse. The turning of the seasons serves as a potent metaphor in many Jones and Schmidt shows, and in this 1960 classic, young love and friendship are examined against the inevitable changing climes. *The Fantasticks* is their shining example and a perfect small musical.

2. *FALSETTOS*

William Finn and James Lapine's teaming of two musicals in Finn's "Marvin" trilogy, *March of the Falsettos* and *Falsettoland*. These two shows (and their predecessor, *In Trousers*) tell the story of a married father's struggles to come to terms with his latent homosexuality. The shifting definitions of "family" are examined in these shows; none has a cast larger than seven (one character even makes note of the "teeny tiny band" playing for them). *March* and *Falsettoland* were first paired for a full evening in 1992 by director-choreographer Graciela Daniele at Hartford Stage Company.

3. *MARRY ME A LITTLE*

This chamber musical was conceived by then-budding playwright Craig Lucas (*Prelude to a Kiss*, *Longtime Companion*) to fill a late-night slot off-off-Broadway back in 1981. Stephen Sondheim gave his blessing to the use of eighteen of his "trunk" songs, songs cut from other shows. The two-character, one-piano evening told the interesting tale of two lonely souls living in separate apartments, yet inhabiting the same stage space, articulating their hopes and dreams through Sondheim's songs.

4. *I DO! I DO!*

The always-experimental Tom Jones and Harvey Schmidt cast two of Broadway's biggest stars, Robert Preston and Mary Martin, as the entire cast, a married couple, in their 1966 musical based on Jan de Hartog's play *The Fourposter*. *I Do! I Do!* was an examination of a marriage in music, and Preston and Martin, despite having to carry the whole show, predictably filled the entire theater with their warmth and sheer star power.

5. *AIN'T MISBEHAVIN'*

Off-off-Broadway all the way to Tony Awards and a legendary run and reputation, all for a cabaret show about a stride piano player. 1977's *Ain't Misbehavin'* successfully and ebulliently recreated the spirit and the music of the legendary Fats Waller, with a cast of just five strutting in high style, backed by a piano player (the great Luther Henderson at the show's premiere) and a small jazz combo.

6. *john & jen*

The two-performer, three-person-orchestra chamber show *john & jen* came to off-Broadway in 1995 by way of the venerable Goodspeed Opera House, birthplace of many shows, both large and small. But *john & jen* took a novel approach to its subject matter, the changing dynamics of love, families, and sacrifice, as one actress played jen to one actor playing her brother, john, and his son, also called john. Papa john is killed in Vietnam, and jen must connect to young john in order to bring their grief and understanding full circle.

7. *BABY*

An agreeable but somewhat banal 1983 musical about a potentially interesting subject. *Baby* concerns three couples (in their forties, thirties, and twenties) and their adventures in the baby game. As each couple tries to conceive, they must confront not only impending parenthood, but also the demands placed on their relationships with each other. The book, by Sybille Pearson, covered this territory better than Richard Maltby, Jr. and David Shire's mediocre score.

8. *THE LaST FIVE YEaRS*

Another two-hander, this time from the pen of the talented Jason Robert Brown, who wrote book, music, and lyrics. *The Last 5 Years* depicts the five-year relationship of Jamie and Cathy, examining their time together by playing that time backwards, starting with the breakup of their marriage and ending with their first entrancing meeting. Brown cleverly orchestrates their relationship, nowhere better than in the final numbers, "Goodbye Until Tomorrow/I Could Never Rescue You," which juxtaposes their first goodbye (after their first date) with their last.

9. *GOBLIN MaRKET*

Christina Rossetti's allegorical poem *Goblin Market* was adapted into a two-character musical at the tiny Vineyard Theater in 1985. The allegory is mainly sexual, as two sisters visit their childhood nursery and find their memories invaded by goblins and the forbidden fruits they bear. Peggy Harmon and Polly Pen made a quite unusual verse musical out of this material, with actresses Ann Morrison and Terri Klausner hauntingly portraying the sisters.

10. *THREE POSTCaRDS*

Singer-songwriter Craig Carnelia is often referred to as the musical theater's best-kept secret. Or used to be, anyway, before *Sweet Smell of Success* bombed so loudly on Broadway. But before *Success* smelled, off-Broadway lauded his superb *Three Postcards*, from 1986. Three women meet for lunch in a trendy bistro, to the tinkling sounds of our orchestra, the bistro's piano player. The only other character is the pithy waiter, who frequently interrupts the ladies' reveries.

It's an Art

10 Musicals about Other Art Forms

Musicals often hold a fun-house mirror up to nature, distorting real life by musicalizing it. Here are ten musicals about other parts of the fun house—different types of show business.

1. *BARNUM*

Cy Coleman, Mark Bramble, and Michael Stewart's 1980 musical biography of the legendary showman P. T. Barnum. Director and choreographer Joe Layton wisely set the evening within the context of a circus, with a ringmaster announcing the scenes. Orchestrator Hershy Kay and set designer David Mitchell made invaluable contributions to the three-ring evening.

2. *MY FAVORITE YEAR*

The hectic, seat-of-the-pants world of early variety television gets the once-over in this unsuccessful musical from 1992. Adapted from the 1982 film of the same name, *My Favorite Year* concerns a young gofer working on the King Kaiser television show who is assigned to babysit a dipsomaniacal matinee idol prior to his appearance on the show. An appealing cast did their best but the atmosphere was never convincingly portrayed.

3.   *3 GUYS NAKED FROM THE WAIST DOWN*

No, it's not a porn musical. "Naked from the waist down" is trade lingo for stand-up comics, who let it all hang out for everyone to see when they step to the mike. This 1985 off-Broadway show follows the parallel lives of three comics, starting in small clubs and aiming for the big time (Heeeeeeere's Johnny!) and the very different paths their lives take. Loud, bombastic rock-and-roll storytelling was the order of the day.

4.   *CITY OF ANGELS*

A best-selling detective novelist adapting his work into a Hollywood film is the subject of this very funny, superbly conceived 1989 musical. Larry Gelbart's book portrays both the real, "color" world of the writer up against the Hollywood system, and the *noir* world of his characters, in black and white, sometimes both on-stage at once. Even more ingenious was the use of the same actors to portray the real people as well as their fictional counterparts, daring the audience to decide which bunch was more unsavory. Cy Coleman and David Zippel's score was one of the best of the 1980s, and saw out the decade in excellent style.

5.   *DREAMGIRLS*

1981's *Dreamgirls* was an intriguing show in concept— the tale of the rise and fall of the Dreams, a girl group obviously based on the Supremes—but just a mediocre show on paper. Michael Bennett cast the show with performers who sold the R & B style to the hilt. Bennett's legendary staging literally never stopped moving, and the non-stop dancing was aided greatly by lightning-fast costume changes and scenic designer

The 1989 musical *City of Angels,* written by Larry Gelbart, Cy Coleman, and David Zippel, was a jazzy and wickedly funny spoof on film noir.

Robin Wagner's amazing movable light towers, which seemed to dance themselves.

6. *THE 1940'S RADIO HOUR*

An evening-long spoof of the days of post-depression live radio broadcasts, this show takes place in a radio studio, and we meet seemingly the entire radio station over the course of the evening. The show's clever structure includes using the pit band as the studio orchestra, a sound effects man, and actual product jingles and songs from the period. The very funny "Eskimo Pies" commercial is among the most popular audition pieces for actresses.

7. *THE RED SHOES*

This legendary 1994 Broadway flop is based on the classic film *Ninotchka*. Composer Jule Styne and author Marsha Norman came up with an adaptation which veered wildly in tone, suffered from too much tampering in production, and couldn't live up to the legendary film source. Despite effectively choreographed ballet sequences, *The Red Shoes* was D.O.A. when it opened and quickly became the latest in a depressingly long string of high-profile flops.

8. *GYPSY*

Very loosely based on striptease queen Gypsy Rose Lee's autobiographical memoir of her days in burlesque, *Gypsy* is one of the very best musicals ever written. Arthur Laurents' book concentrates not on Lee and her sister, June Hovic, better known as June Havoc, but rather on their stage mother from hell, Rose.

Rose, as delineated by Laurents, Jule Styne, and Stephen Sondheim (and thrillingly and terrifyingly embodied by Ethel Merman), was a near-heartless Gorgon living vicariously through her "babies," pushing them headfirst into show business and not capable of letting go when her babies outgrow her smothering protection.

9. *ONE TOUCH OF VENUS*

"New art is true art," says Whitelaw Savory, patron of the new and fresh. But in *One Touch of Venus*, Savory buys a mysterious ancient statue of Venus, which comes to life via the touch (and engagement ring) of a Manhattan barber. Eventually, the statue vanishes then reappears, spreading her message of pleasure and liberation all over Manhattan island.

S.J. Perelman and Ogden Nash's libretto sets the witty show in motion, and the Nash-Kurt Weill score takes it from there. Classics like "Speak Low" and "Westwind" jostle for position with private-eye shenanigans and crazy chases in this gorgeous, funny 1944 take on modern art and timeless love.

10. *THE GREAT WALTZ*

The Great Waltz examines the middle age of the Waltz King, Johann Strauss, Sr. and his increasingly volatile relationship with his son, Johann Jr., who later became *his* generation's Waltz King. Their mutual respect and understanding is finally cemented when Senior conducts the premiere performance of Junior's "On the Beautiful Blue Danube."

Cobbled together by Robert Wright and George Forrest for the Long Beach Civic Light Opera, *The Great Waltz* boasts an all-Strauss score, often set to unimaginative lyrics. The silly book often sets these tunes in unfortunately preposterous situations. In all, it's neither Broadway caliber nor a fitting tribute to either Strauss.

Children Will Listen
Parents and Children
in the Musical Theater

Many parents want their children to step into the family business, but many people in show business wouldn't wish their careers on anyone, least of all their offspring. Luckily for us, some of the theater's leading lights let their genes have their way.

1. SHIRLEY JONES/JACK CASSIDY AND DAVID, SHAUN, AND PATRICK CASSIDY

Jack Cassidy was a handsome smoothie who turned in a memorable performance as no-goodnik Stephen Kodaly in *She Loves Me*. Jones was a beautiful ingenue who, after making her Broadway debut as a replacement Laurey in *Oklahoma!*, went Hollywood debuting in Fred Zinneman's film version.

Their three sons have all appeared on Broadway, teen-pop idols David and Shaun appearing together in the musical *Blood Brothers* (as twins) in 1994. Youngest son Patrick made his Broadway debut in 1982 and appeared most recently opposite Cheryl Ladd in the hit revival of *Annie Get Your Gun*.

2. **CARLIN GLYNN AND MARY STUART MASTERSON**

Glynn is the warm, attractive leading lady who won a Tony in 1979 (wisely billed in the "Featured Actress" category, otherwise she would have been steamrolled by Angela Lansbury and the *Sweeney Todd* juggernaut) for her performance as Mona Stangley in *The Best Little Whorehouse in Texas*, which was co-authored by her husband, Peter Masterson.

Their daughter Mary Stuart, best known for her performances in films like *Fried Green Tomatoes* and *Benny and Joon*, appeared on Broadway in Eva LaGallienne's adaptation-with-music of *Alice in Wonderland*, and was seen as Luisa in the Roundabout Theater's recent revival of *Nine*.

3. **RICHARD RODGERS AND MARY RODGERS GUETTEL**

Broadway's greatest composer rarely made mistakes in his illustrious career, but his daughter Mary said she became interested in composing because the mistakes she made playing the piano were often more intriguing than what had actually been written. She learned her lessons well, composing a superb score at the tender age of 28 for *Once Upon a Mattress*. She now serves as head of the Rodgers and Hammerstein Organization, which licenses the work of her father.

Another spin of the wheel: Her son, Adam Guettel, is one of the handful of the "new breed" of theater composers. He wrote the very successful off-Broadway musical *Floyd Collins* and the popular song cycle *Saturn Returns*.

4. **HAROLD AND DAISY PRINCE**

No one has more Tony Awards than Broadway's own royal, Harold Prince. Prince worked his way up from assistant stage manager on *Call Me Madam* in 1950 to an unparalleled career as a producer and director of such legendary shows as *West Side Story*, *Company*, *Sweeney Todd*, and *The Phantom of the Opera*.

One of the few missteps in his career was Stephen Sondheim and George Furth's flop *Merrily We Roll Along* in 1981. *Merrily* featured Prince Hal's daughter, Daisy Prince, making her Broadway debut as Meg, girlfriend of Franklin Shepard, the show's antihero. Miss Prince also appeared as Young Phyllis in the legendary *Follies in Concert* and has carved out a career of her own as a successful off-Broadway director of shows like *The Last Five Years* and *Songs for a New World*. In 1994, she appeared at the Public Theater in a fractured fairy tale of a musical called *The Petrified Prince* . . . directed by her father.

5.   RICHARD AND KATE BURTON

Richard Burton, the immortal Welshman, gave one of the musical theater's most commanding performances as King Arthur in Lerner and Loewe's *Camelot*. (Burton was so good as Arthur that, upon reviving it in 1980, one critic wondered why Guinevere ever would have left *him*.)

His daughter Kate made her Broadway musical debut three years later as J.J. in the short-lived musical version of Garry Trudeau's comic strip *Doonesbury*, and later appeared in the high-profile Broadway revival of Stephen Sondheim's *Company* as karate-fighting Sarah. In 2002, she was nominated for two straight play Tony Awards, for *The Elephant Man* and *Hedda Gabler*, the latter produced by her mother, Sybil Christopher.

6. OSCAR II AND JAMES AND WILLIAM HAMMERSTEIN

Some consider Oscar Hammerstein to be the MVP of the Broadway musical (considering his contributions to two of the linchpin shows, *Show Boat* and *Oklahoma!* as well as his other classics), and his two sons, James and William, had admirable careers of their own on Broadway, and on the road, as producers and directors of renown.

Most famously, James served as co-director of the Broadway incarnation of his father's *State Fair* in 1996, while William's most notable project was the well-received major Broadway revival of *Oklahoma!* in 1979, which he directed.

7. BOB FOSSE/GWEN VERDON AND NICOLE FOSSE

One of the greatest onstage pairings in Broadway history was the teaming of the slick, seductive choreography and direction of Bob Fosse and the performances of his longtime wife and muse, the dazzling redheaded singer/dancer Gwen Verdon. The work of the two shone in shows like *Sweet Charity*, *Redhead*, and *Chicago*, Verdon oozing talent, class, and sex appeal, all shown off to maximum effect by Fosse's riveting staging.

Their daughter Nicole made her Broadway debut as a member of the *corps de ballet* of the "Opera Populaire" in *The Phantom of the Opera*. She danced for her father in his 1979 film *All That Jazz* and appeared as Kristine in the movie version of *A Chorus Line*. Both mother and daughter served in consulting positions on *Fosse*, the Tony-winning tribute to the late choreographer.

8. JAMES AND MATTHEW BRODERICK

The late stage and television actor James Broderick made his Broadway debut in 1953 in the musical *Maggie,* loosely based on J.M. Barrie's play *What Every Woman Knows*, which ran a meager five performances. James's son Matthew, however, has fared slightly better in his forays into the Broadway musical.

Matthew's first Broadway musical outing, the 1995 revival *of How to Succeed in Business Without Really Trying*, proved him to be a fine musical farceur and a pretty good singer, winning him his second Tony (his first was for Neil Simon's play *Brighton Beach Memoirs*). As musical farces go, 2001's *The Producers* is Grade-A, and Broderick took the role of mousy accountant-turned-crooked-producer Leo Bloom and ran with it, winning raves and audience love letters.

9. LUCILLE BALL/DESI ARNAZ AND LUCIE ARNAZ

The legendary comic pairing of Lucy and Desi yielded a great television series, but the beloved performers had only one Broadway musical apiece, his being Rodgers and Hart's *Too Many Girls* in 1939, hers being Cy Coleman and Carolyn Leigh's *Wildcat* in 1960, when she was at the height of her TV popularity (and, incidentally, the end of her marriage to Arnaz).

Daughter Lucie shot to stardom in 1979 in her Broadway debut, the Neil Simon/ Carole Bayer Sager/ Marvin Hamlisch musical *a clef They're Playing Our Song*. It won her a Tony nomination for her performance as Sager's alter ego, a lovably ditzy lyricist.

10. ZERO AND JOSH MOSTEL

One of the legendary clowns (a "superclown," as critic Marilyn Stasio described him), Zero Mostel's immense talent, appetite, and ego made him one of the American theater's true characters. A three-time Tony winner, two of those awards were for memorable musical creations: Pseudolus, the wily slave in *A Funny Thing Happened on the Way to the Forum*, and his remarkable Tevye in *Fiddler on the Roof.*

Following an unfortunate experience working with his father on a television show while in college, Josh Mostel struck out on a successful career of his own, albeit mostly in "fat clown" roles like those played by his father. Also like his father, Josh appeared in two Broadway musicals: the 1990 revival of *3 Penny Opera*, and as Sy Benson in the short-lived *My Favorite Year*. Unlike his father, who was often considered too "outsized" for the movies, Josh has had a long and successful film career, one of his most memorable performances coming in his movie debut as the libertine King Herod in *Jesus Christ Superstar.*

Keep It Gay
10 Musicals with, Um, Happy Bachelor Characters

The musical theater is created, performed, and attended by an overwhelming number of gay men and women. Odd, then, that so much of the gay content in earlier musicals was completely coded (just look at almost any Cole Porter lyric, for example). There still aren't many gay-themed shows with gay characters in them. Here are ten shows with important homosexual content.

1. *LADY IN THE DARK*

A masterpiece of storytelling as well as subtext, *Lady in the Dark* is a supremely innovative and heavily sexually coded musical about inner crises and personal triumph. It also featured one of the first sympathetic gay characters in Broadway history.

Lady in the Dark's libretto was written by Moss Hart, a gay man who was, at the time, married to a woman. His heroine is Liza Elliott, a magazine editor in personal and professional crises, afraid of her inner demons. While this is obvious subtext for a gay man's self-loathing, the only openly gay character in the show, photographer Russell Paxton, is a trusted confidante to Liza (he also gets a lot of great music, like the tongue-twisting "Tschaikowsky").

2. *HOWARD CRABTREE'S WHOOP-DEE-DOO!*

This one is, as the title suggests, a plotless revue. But come on, that's one of the funniest show titles you'll ever see, so here it is in this book. *Whoop-Dee-Doo!* was mainly the brainchild of the aforementioned Howard Crabtree, who wrote a bit, performed a bit, produced a bit, and designed all of the costumes.

The show itself was a teeny *Follies*-style revue on gay themes, with songs like "Tough to Be a Fairy," "I Was Born This Way," and "Nancy, the Unauthorized Musical." (Wonder who *that's* about.) Crabtree's costumes, which often defied description and were worth the price of admission alone, stole the show.

3. *KISS OF THE SPIDER WOMAN*

Manuel Puig's political play had been adapted into a 1985 film by Hector Babenco which won William Hurt an Academy Award. Hurt played Molina, a gay window dresser imprisoned for lewd acts, who is confined with Valentin, a political dissident, in a hellish South American prison.

The great songwriting team of Kander and Ebb, along with librettist Terrence McNally, adapted *Spider Woman* into a musical in 1990, and it finally hit Broadway in the Spring of 1993. Molina, played movingly by Tony winner Brent Carver, must get close to Valentin for reasons of survival, but their bond eventually becomes genuine. Molina's relationships with Valentin and, especially, his own mother (epitomized in the song "You Could Never Shame Me"), are heartbreakingly real and touching.

4. *THE MARVIN SONGS*

Composer-lyricist-librettist William Finn wrote, between 1979 and 1990, three very original, very angry musical theater pieces that have become known, in trilogy, as "The Marvin Songs." They deal with Marvin, a married father, who leaves his wife and son for another man.

That's the first show, *In Trousers*. 1981's *March of the Falsettos* details Marvin's relationship with his lover, Whizzer, and Marvin's wife, Trina, and her relationship with the family's psychiatrist, Mendel. 1990's *Falsettoland* brings the trilogy full circle as Whizzer faces AIDS and Jason, Marvin's son, deals with his impending manhood via his bar mitzvah. Selfish, insecure, passionate Marvin and the other characters that form this extended family are not saints or sinners, but rather brilliantly human, thanks to Finn's skillful, iconoclastic writing.

5. *AVENUE Q*

Broadway's freshest new hit (2003) looks to be the off-Broadway transfer (from the Vineyard Theater) *Avenue Q*. A post-modern spin on sexual identity and acceptance, the show, about Princeton, a young man who moves into a brownstone on the titular street, is presented in a tongue-in-cheek, *Sesame Street* style. Including the puppets.

Ah, the puppets. *Avenue Q*'s gimmick is that our hero encounters many characters along his not-exactly-G-rated journey, and many of them are life-size puppets. One of them is the straight-arrow (hah!) Rod, who is proud of his Republicanism and staunchly declares "I am not a closeted homowhatever!" Whatever, Rod. When puppet Lucy T. Slut is jockeying for stage time with a woman playing Gary Coleman, the puppet's closeted homosexuality seems almost normal.

6. *CHICAGO*

"When you're good to Mama," sings Matron Mama Morton in her big number in *Chicago*, "Mama's good to you." *Chicago,* adapted in 1975 from Maurine Dallas Watkins's 1926 play of the same name, is a completely cynical examination of celebrity and crime. And riding herd over the Merry Murderesses in Cook County Jail is Matron Mama Morton.

Mama is, not to put too fine a point on it, a bull-dyke who knows her position and plays it to the hilt. As played on Broadway originally by great old character gal Mary McCarty, and in revival by Marcia Lewis (and, for the record, too warmly and sexily by Queen Latifah in the movie), her randy attitude towards her girls is perfectly in keeping with the robust cynicism of the musical.

7. *A CHORUS LINE*

One of Broadway's greatest musicals, *A Chorus Line* is often accused of being too emotionally cold and aloof in its telling the tale of a dancers' audition which becomes, by extension, an encounter session. A dancers' encounter session actually fueled the conception of *A Chorus Line*, with dancers of every stripe telling their stories on tape.

One of those stories came from gay dancer Nicholas Dante, who eventually shared co-authorship of the book, whose moving tale of his adolescence spent dancing in drag clubs was inserted almost wholesale into *A Chorus Line* and given to the character Paul. Paul's monologue is one of many non-dancing set pieces that give this superbly constructed musical its heart.

8. *YOUR OWN THING*

There is, in the canons of musical theater lore, a serious dearth of satisfactory musical versions of Shakespeare. One of the very best is a swingin' late-sixties adaptation of Shakespeare's *Twelfth Night*. John Driver, Hal Hester, and Danny Apolinar's long-running off-Broadway hit *Your Own Thing* cheerfully embraces the free-wheeling gender politics of the original Shakespeare and twists them in groovy psychedelic style.

Your Own Thing follows a confused Viola into Illyria, aka N.Y.C., where she meets her Orson and must disguise herself as a man to gain entrance into his nightclub's house band. Her disguise fools him into thinking she's a he, which he digs more than he would if she were a she and not a he. Tuneful (and, considering it's a Shakespeare adaptation, surprisingly topical) comedy follows until everybody notices the show's title and realizes what bag they're into.

9. *THE FAGGOT*

Although he's still alive, Al Carmines is something of a secret in the world of musical theater. A practicing minister as well as a gay man, Carmines, whose congregation is in New York's West Village, was greatly influenced by the free-for-all nature of the Living Theater movement of the late '60s, and in 1973, The Truck and Warehouse Theater presented his off-Broadway revue *The Faggot*.

The Faggot was a collection of songs presented in semi-oratorio style, neither preachy nor campy. Rather, the songs were basically vignettes of ordinary gay and lesbian life, occasionally explicit (such as in "The Hustler," which was basically a pickup in song), but never tasteless or whiny. Carmines won Obie Awards for *The Faggot*, but, predictably, it achieved no commercial success.

10. *La CaGE auX FOLLES*

Adapted from the French farce of the same name (spun off into two hit films as well), Jerry Herman and Harvey Fierstein's *La Cage aux Folles* is a simple tale of unconditional love with a mild twist: Both lead characters are gay, and one has a son who wishes to marry a girl. Of course, her parents are completely out-of-touch with the gay lifestyle, and in true French farce form, must debase themselves, and cross-dress, to escape scandal.

The gay couple are more well-adjusted, although not completely without faults: Albin, the "wife" of the couple, is a perpetual worrywart who is only secure as a performer (his moment of truth comes in the stirring anthem "I Am What I Am," in which he proudly declares his effeminate homosexuality). His lover, Georges, the "masculine" one, is the soothing, calm presence in the relationship, gently reassuring his lover in "Song on the Sand" and scolding his wayward son in "Look Over There."

Where Did We Go Right?

10 Surprise Hit Musicals

"**N**O LEGS NO JOKES NO CHANCE" read the telegram Walter Winchell's secretary cabled back to New York from New Haven, after seeing a preview of *Away We Go!* That show became *Oklahoma!*, an American institution. Here are ten musicals that became successful surprises.

1. *THE FANTASTICKS*

Tom Jones and Harvey Schmidt's tiny off-Broadway tale of young love and the changes of time, adapted from Rostand's *Les Romanesques*, opened in 1960 at the Sullivan Street playhouse and then closed—in 2002. Critics liked it from the start, but nobody expected this little show to become the longest run of its kind in American theater history. Of course, it helps if you can write songs like "Try to Remember" and "Soon It's Gonna Rain."

2. *ME AND MY GIRL*

A prewar hit in London, *Me and My Girl* was the purely British musical-comedy story of a Cockney busker who inherits a title but still wants to marry his commoner girlfriend. When it was revived and brought to Broadway in 1986, *Me and My Girl* provided some relief from the Brit-pop spectacles overwhelming both sides of the Atlantic in the mid-'80s.

Composer-lyricist Noel Gay's son, Richard Armitage, took a risk in producing the show in London in 1985, and, thanks to creative script and score revisions and the mighty hand of director Mike Ockrent, the show hit big in London and unearthed two major stars in Emma Thompson and Robert Lindsay, the latter of whom won a Tony when the show triumphed on Broadway.

3. *Sarafina!*

A South African export courtesy of New York's Lincoln Center, *Sarafina!* was the brainchild of Mbongeni Ngema, who wrote the show with the great trumpeter and composer Hugh Masekela and directed it as well. A "township jive" musical about the immediate effects of apartheid on South African schoolchildren, *Sarafina!* was written in an indigenous style known as mbanqa. The youthful cast, delivering the musical's message of inexorable change with irresistible spirit, traveled all the way from South Africa to Lincoln Center's off-Broadway Newhouse Theater to Broadway's Cort Theater in the 1987–88 season.

4. *Hair*

America's "tribal love-rock musical" started at the New York Shakespeare Festival's Public Theater off-Broadway in 1967. It was cited downtown as a powerful portrait of youth flying in the face of an unpopular war, with kudos going to composer Galt MacDermot, author-actors Gerome Ragni and James Rado, and director Gerald Freedman.

Michael Butler produced the show when it moved to

Broadway later that season, firing Freedman and hiring Tom O'Horgan, then a hot name in experimental circles, to direct. Perhaps not trusting the inherent sincerity of the piece, O'Horgan tarted it up, blowing the honest sentiments up and out of context and making it The Revolution, Televised. The resulting version of *Hair*, on Broadway, became the first counterculture hit on the Main Stem.

5. *AIN'T MISBEHAVIN'*

Director Richard Maltby, Jr. conceived this evening of songs in tribute to stride piano giant Fats Waller for Manhattan Theater Club's tiny cabaret space off-off-Broadway in 1977. Within weeks, word was out: This was the "little show that could" for the season. Selling out downtown, the small show (featuring just five performers and a jazz combo) moved uptown and ritzed itself up in time to win the Tony for Best Musical. Generally hailed as the best songwriter revue in Broadway history, its opening night cast (the Protean quintet of Charlaine Woodard, Ken Page, Armelia McQueen, Andre de Shields, and Nell Carter) is also regularly cited as the best ever for a small show.

6. *ON YOUR TOES*

A show which was, in many ways, ahead of its time in 1936 became a sleeper hit in a 1983 revival which, somehow, opened under Broadway's radar. Perhaps the previous revival, in 1954, soured some on the show's reputation.

On Your Toes was a conventional Rodgers and Hart musical comedy with three, count 'em, three, ballets socked into it. A typically elephantine 1930s plot, concerning Russian ballerinas, a music teacher, vaudevillians, and hitmen jostles with the classic song score,

Martha Swope and Lara Teeter

In 1983, the revival of Rodgers and Hart's 1936 musical, *On Your Toes,* became a sleeper hit of the season. Pictured here, singing the classic, "There's a Small Hotel," are the wonderful Christine Andreas (left) and Lara Teeter.

which includes "Glad to be Unhappy" and the all-timer "There's a Small Hotel."

The 1983 revival was praised by critics for its respect of the show's basic elements. Unlike recent revivals, which often earn the sobriquet "revisals," this revival had no overweening concepts applied to it. Perhaps that's because the master, Mr. George Abbott, and original orchestrator, Hans Spialek, were around to make sure that the musical comedy was just that. The ballets, notably the jazzy-classical "Slaughter on Tenth Avenue," were treated like gold (and danced that way, too).

7. *GREASE*

Chicago's legendary Kingston Mines blues club was, inexplicably, the incubator for this cheerful doo-wop Valentine. Without winning a single Tony Award, the show managed to stay afloat on powerful word-of-mouth and survived to become the longest running Broadway musical of its time.

Basically, the plot of *Grease* comes across as the anti-Pygmalion—be a skank and you'll get the guy of your dreams—but following a hit run in 1971 off-Broadway at Entermedia, *Grease* went on to Broadway's Royale Theater, where it stayed for 3,388 cheerfully skanky performances.

8. *NUNSENSE*

Dan Goggin wrote and directed this small show about a group of nuns trying to raise money to bury one of their own. It's a talent show (taking place on their school's set of *Grease*, no less) which soon becomes a mystery. Where did the missing nun go? Why does one of them have a nun puppet?

So, okay, singing, dancing nuns *are* pretty funny. This 1985 show rode that mild taboo to become an overwhelming success, running at New York's Cherry Lane Theater for almost nine years, spawning countless productions worldwide and several sequels. Dan Goggins probably owns the building in which you're reading this book.

9. *URINETOWN*

April 2001 saw the premiere of this small satire of big business off-Broadway at the teeny Chernuchin Theater, where it became a hit among the *Entertainment Weekly* set for its cheeky satire, its gentle mocking of showbiz conventions, and the fact that it was called *Urinetown*. (You're in town? Yes, I am, what's your point? Wait. You mean . . . oh.)

Prior to September 11, a Broadway transfer was announced, then delayed, but *Urinetown* finally made it to the big time (and three Tony Awards) in fall 2001. As the nation reeled, smart comedies were what Broadway audiences seemed to want, and *Urinetown* filled the bill.

10. *LITTLE MARY SUNSHINE*

In the wilderness of the off-Broadway of the 1950s, occasionally a big hit popped up, most notably the Theater de Lys production of *The Threepenny Opera* and Rick Besoyan's *Little Mary Sunshine*. Besoyan's 1959 spoof was entirely his creation—book, music, and lyrics—and came out of absolutely nowhere.

A very, very campy spoof of operettas, most notably Rudolf Friml's Mountie epic *Rose Marie*, the tongue-in-cheek *Little Mary Sunshine* cost virtually nothing to put on and starred no one famous at the time (Oscar-nominee-to-be Eileen Brennan played Little Mary) and rode a wave of critical raves to a then rare 1,143 performances off-Broadway.

Am I My Resumé?
Musical Actors Who Write

As any stage actor will tell you, there's no money in acting on the stage. Actors will also tell you they're biding their time until that perfect part written just for them comes along. Here are ten performers who got tired of waiting and wrote—some parts for themselves, some for their colleagues.

1. SIR NOEL COWARD

England's legendary wit was represented on Broadway many times over as an author of both straight plays and musicals. His skills as a composer-lyricist occasionally ran toward the twee, but he was also capable of writing music of devastating beauty, as in his 1934 Broadway operetta *Bitter Sweet*, which contains the haunting "If You Could Only Come With Me."

2. MICHAEL RUPERT

First, Mike Rupert was a Broadway juvenile in musicals like 1968's *The Happy Time*. In the '80s, he became a Tony winner for *Sweet Charity* and the definitive "Marvin" in William Finn's *Falsettos* trilogy. In 1984, he wrote the music for the successful stand-up comedy musical *3 Guys Naked from the Waist Down* and the music for and starred in the 1988 Broadway flop *Mail*, about a man whose mail comes to life.

3. MELVIN VAN PEEBLES

In addition to being a powerful filmmaker and actor (*Sweet Sweetback's Baad Asssss Song*), Melvin van Peebles wrote, directed, produced, and starred in a bunch of musicals, most interestingly *Ain't Supposed to Die a Natural Death*, a bitter, pointed inner city screed, and *Don't Play Us Cheap!*, a hopeful counter-point piece to *Natural Death*. That both these musicals were seen on Broadway in one season (1971–72) is testament to Melvin van Peebles' gifts as a musical artist.

4. GEORGE M. COHAN

When it comes to the American musical, you name it and George M. Cohan did it. And probably did it more times than anyone else. From the 1901 musical *The Governor's Son* to *Little Johnny Jones* a few years later, through *The Tavern* and *Little Nellie Kelly*, and ending with *I'd Rather Be Right* over thirty years later, George M. Cohan *was* the American musical, as author, composer, lyricist, director, actor, theater owner, and producer.

5. JAMES RADO, GEROME RAGNI

These two came as a package deal. In the tumultuous season of 1967–1968, *Hair* changed a lot of peoples' minds about what musical theater could be, and James Rado and Gerome Ragni authored *Hair* (along with composer Galt MacDermot) and played soldier boy

Claude and hippie tribe leader Berger, respectively. Hair opened at the Public Theater off-Broadway, then hit Broadway's Biltmore Theater by way of the Cheetah nightclub.

6. HARVEY FIERSTEIN

Gravel-voiced Fierstein is the current toast of Broadway for his cross-dressing performance in the smash musical *Hairspray*. Fierstein, the author of the Tony Award-winning play *Torch Song Trilogy*, also won a 1983 Tony for his book for the musical *La Cage aux Folles*. Flop collectors love him for his book for the 1988 mega-bomb *Legs Diamond*.

7. JOHN CAMERON MITCHELL

Mitchell is another popular performer in both the musical and non-musical genres; his musical credits in New York include Broadway's very conventional *The Secret Garden* and the more experimental *Hello Again* off-Broadway at Lincoln Center. But Mitchell's biggest triumph has come as the author and star of the rock musical *Hedwig and The Angry Inch*, which he made into a popular film as well. Both theater and rock types look forward to his next move.

8. LONNY PRICE

Long respected as a musical actor (*Merrily We Roll Along, Rags*) and director (*Juno* off-Broadway, the new *Urban Cowboy*), Lonny Price finally branched into musical authorship with *A Class Act* in 2001. *A Class Act,* for which Price also directed and starred, is the affectionate biography of the late Edward Kleban, a prolific songwriter best known as lyricist for *A Chorus Line*.

9.   NICHOLAS DANTE

One of Kleban's collaborators on the groundbreaking
A Chorus Line, former chorus dancer Nick Dante was
present at the legendary taping sessions in 1974 which
served as inspiration for the dance project that eventually evolved into the smash hit. His involvement with
and commitment to the project was such that eventually Michael Bennett asked him to co-author the book
to *A Chorus Line,* which won Dante the Pulitzer Prize
and Tony award, as well as just about every other theater award imaginable.

10.   WALTER BOBBIE

Starting in 1971, with *Frank Merriwell*, Walter Bobbie
was a reliable musical performer who created the role
of Roger in the smash *Grease*, as well as Nicely-Nicely
Johnson in the 1992 revival of *Guys and Dolls*. In
1994, he conceived and directed the Rodgers and
Hammerstein revue *A Grand Night for Singing*, which
led to his helming the long-running revival of *Chicago*.
Most recently, in 1999, Bobbie co-adapted, with Dean
Pitchford, and directed the movie musical *Footloose* for
Broadway.

I Saw Stars

Recent TV Shows with Tony Winners and Nominees

Once, a Broadway star would take New York by storm, then they'd be whisked away to Hollywood and the movies. Now, the quick riches and notoriety of TV are often the big lure. Some good, some bad below.

1. ***ENCORE! ENCORE!***

Funnyman Nathan Lane was given his shot at sitcom stardom with this 1998 NBC offering, about an opera singer who loses his voice, then returns home to his family's Napa Valley wine orchards to begin his life anew. Most pegged this one as a winner. Then the cameras started rolling.

Troubled from the start, *Encore! Encore!* hit the airwaves in the fall of 1998 with very little network support and unwisely featured Lane playing *Frasier*-type high comedy instead of his trademark comic desperation. It was one of the high-profile disasters of the season. Lane got a second chance with a new sitcom about a gay actor who runs for Congress, which was also unsuccessful.

2. *KRISTIN*

Pint-sized tornado Kristin Chenoweth made a big hit on Broadway in *You're a Good Man, Charlie Brown*, for which she won a 1999 Tony. Her squeaky-voiced portrayal of Sally Brown eventually led her fortunes to NBC, who spent a year and a half putting *Kristen* on the air.

The dreadful summer 2001 replacement show featured Chenoweth as Kristin Yancey, typical plucky aide to your typical idiotic corporate blowhole. The squeaky voice was still there, but, like everything in this stupid sitcom turkey, was misguided. It worked on Broadway because she played a *four-year-old*, fellas.

3. *THE MARTIN SHORT SHOW*

After his Tony-winning stint in 1998's *Little Me*, the comic genius Martin Short waded into the risky waters of the TV talk show. Perhaps Short was hoping to snag some of Rosie O'Donnell's Broadway-happy audience, but his eponymous show went the way of approximately 99.95 percent of all talk shows.

Short's chameleonesque aptitude for creating sketch characters gave the show its one saving grace: the grotesquely comic Hollywood columnist Jiminy Glick, who now has his own show on Comedy Central (*Primetime Glick*). As of this writing, Short is knocking 'em dead in Los Angeles in *The Producers*.

4. *SEINFELD*

One of the most popular sitcoms of all time, *Seinfeld* was built around observational stand-up comic Jerry Seinfeld, but boasted an eclectic supporting cast. Julia Louis-Dreyfus (galpal Elaine) hailed from Chicago's Second City school of improv comedy, Michael Richards (Kramer) was a Los Angeles–based sketch comedy and commercials guy, and Jason Alexander (pathetic George) was a New York musical theater guy.

Alexander won his Tony in 1989 for *Jerome Robbins' Broadway* (he was also in the legendary flop *Merrily We Roll Along* in 1981; no Tony), then headed west and hooked up with the *Seinfeld* crew and the rest is history. And lots of money. He starred with the aforementioned Martin Short in *The Producers* in La-La Land.

5. *HACK*

Two-time Tony winner Donna Murphy (*Passion*, *The King and I*) is gorgeous, funny, and a phenomenal singer and song stylist. So it's no surprise to anybody that she's been badly used by the suits in Hollywood.

Following her triumph as Fosca in Stephen Sondheim's *Passion* in 1994, she guested as Francesca Cross on the thriller *Murder One* on ABC starting in 1995. Many uninspiring (and, naturally, non-musical) movies followed, broken up by another Tony for *The King and I* in 1996, until the sitcom misfire *What About Joan* in 2001. (At least she got to sing in one episode, and she ripped it up.) She now plays Heather Olshansky on CBS's wildly implausible cop-turned-cabbie series *Hack*.

6. *MISTER STERLING*

An obvious attempt to cash in on the "DC cred" of *The West Wing*, the 2002–2003 NBC series *Mister Sterling* gave the viewer a dashing young senator who speaks his mind and plays it his way, dammit. Lucky for those who watch, it also gives the viewer Audra McDonald as his chief of staff, Jackie Brock.

McDonald is a fiery performer with three Tony Awards to her name, and a growing reputation as a cabaret performer and recording artist. The gig on the cancelled *Mister Sterling* was an attempt for this talented lady to reach the mass audience she deserves.

7. *L.a. FIREFIGHTERS*

Gee, what do you suppose this one was about? A blatant attempt to do for firemen what *ER* did for doctors and *Baywatch* did for lifeguards, *L.A. Firefighters* is looked back upon with absolutely no fondness from anyone. It's particularly unfortunate for musical fans because it cost New York one of its prime hunks, Jarrod Emick.

Emick, a handsome, stocky athletic leading man, won a Tony at age age 25 for his Joe Hardy in the 1994 *Damn Yankees* revival. Unfortunately, his agents whispered in his ear, and two years later, he was cashing Fox Television's checks in the aforementioned *L.A. Firefighters*. Three more bad TV series followed before Emick made it back to New York, as an ideal Brad Majors in *The Rocky Horror Show*. He's slated to play the lover of Peter Allen (Hugh Jackman) in *The Boy From Oz* in late 2003.

8. *NIKKI*

The pneumatic (and actually talented) beauty Nikki Cox was given her own sitcom on the WB network in 2000. The surprisingly-titled *Nikki* was a standard-issue dumb sitcom with one interesting twist: Nikki, our heroine, was a Las Vegas nightclub dancer, and we actually saw at least one production number each episode.

The dancer stuff was the only watchable part of the show, and it was made bearable by the presence of the marvelous Susan Egan as Nikki's randy friend and fellow showgirl, Mary. Egan, a Broadway pro from her days in *Beauty and the Beast* (Tony nomination) and *Triumph of Love* (as well as the superb studio recording of *Drat! The*

Cat!), then *Cabaret*, at least provided some spark to the flop-sweat proceedings. Egan has a lucrative career as a voice-over artist for Japanese *animé* as well.

9. *FAME*

Debbie Allen made a blazing impression on Broadway in the 1980 revival of *West Side Story*, winning a Tony nomination in the process. Alan Parker's semi-documentary *Fame* followed, in which she played a pitiless dance teacher at the New York High School for the Performing Arts. She played the same role, chomping scenery all the way, in the TV version of the movie as well.

Following that was a Tony nomination for the 1986 revival of *Sweet* Charity. The reality TV craze brought Allen and *Fame* back, this time as a bald-faced "talent show" attempt to clone the success of *American Idol*. Allen rides herd on her young charges and pumps them up, shamelessly playing both Simon Cowell and Paula Abdul.

10. *DEAD LIKE ME*

A Tony winner for his thrilling Ché in *Evita*, Broadway favorite Mandy Patinkin has gotten a reputation in recent years as something of an oddity as a performer; indeed, his *Dress Casual* concerts place his singularly committed performances front and center. What's often lost is how truly remarkable an actor he is when he's not the whole damn show.

Following a hilarious, Emmy-nominated cameo as himself on *The Larry Sanders Show,* Patinkin played Dr. Jeffrey Geiger (and won an Emmy) on the CBS medical drama *Chicago Hope*. He now plays Rube, the Grim Reaper—or, more specifically, the father figure to a group of Reapers, soul collectors—on Showtime's offbeat drama *Dead Like Me*.

All We'll Do Is Just Dance
10 Dance Musicals

B roadway musicals usually celebrate the union of spoken word, song, and dance. But in some shows the book and songs go out the window, letting the audience feast primarily on the hoofing. Here are ten shows that gotta dance.

1. *Dancin'*

Bob Fosse eliminated both book and score altogether in this 1978 tribute to the dancers he so dearly loved. *Dancin'* was literally wall-to-wall choreography, saluting ballet, tap, modern dance, jazz dance, and good old Broadway-style hoofing, set to music by artists as diverse as J.S. Bach, Benny Goodman, and Cat Stevens.

2. *Contact*

Director-choreographer Susan Stroman and author John Weidman collaborated on this evening of three dance pieces off-Broadway in 1999. Performed to pre-recorded tracks and featuring no live or original music, *Contact* nevertheless won the Tony Award for Best Musical when it moved to Broadway in 2000. The show was at its best in the third piece, "Contact," which told the tale of a suicidal executive who longs to connect, through dance, with the elusive Girl in the Yellow Dress he sees at a nightclub. The need for communication, for contact, both physical and spiritual, as expressed through dance, is at the heart of this superbly executed dance show.

3. *TANGO ARGENTINO*

The creative and producing team of Claudio Segovia and Hector Orezzoli brought *Tango Argentino* to Broadway in 1985, after playing a hit engagement in Paris. Another plotless dance evening, it nevertheless caused a minor stir due to the sheer physicality and sexiness of the tango dancing on display. Segovia and Orezzoli collaborated on another evening of Hispanic dance, *Flamenco Pura*, and a hit blues revue, *Black and Blue*, in 1989, which won them a Tony for costume design. Choreographer Luis Bravo brought the tango back to Broadway in 1997 with his own evening of Argentine music and dance, *Forever Tango*, and the original show returned to Broadway in 1999.

4. *SWAN LAKE*

Tyro choreographer Matthew Bourne created his *Swan Lake* in London in 1995, the centenary year of the standard Petipa-Ivanov version of Tchaikovsky's classic ballet. Bourne's choreographic conception of the tale of alienation and loneliness featured a black-leather swan, goofy royals, and a gay encounter in a weakling prince's bedroom. The male corps of bare-chested swans created the biggest stir, but despite superb choreography, design, and dancing, most Broadway enthusiasts wondered why it was being treated as a Broadway musical at all. Bourne's concept, radical as it was, didn't disguise the fact that this *Swan Lake* was still a ballet.

5. *JEROME ROBBINS' BROADWAY*

A massive tribute evening to the innovative director-choreographer Jerome Robbins, the 1989 show was directed by Robbins with scenes from virtually all his major work for Broadway, from 1943's *On the Town* to *Funny Girl* in 1964, with many stops in between.

Robbins rehearsed his huge company for the small epoch of nine weeks, during which time he was occasionally seen walking down the street wearing a T-shirt that read, "It's going fine, thank you." All the great moments were included: *West Side Story*'s exquisite suite of ballets, the joyful peasant dances from *Fiddler on the Roof*, the musical-comedy magic of *A Funny Thing Happened on the Way to the Forum* and *Gypsy*, and many others, all woven together as a fitting tribute to one of the architects of the Broadway musical edifice.

6. *BRING IN 'DA NOISE, BRING IN 'DA FUNK*

Perhaps the most innovative musical of the 1990s, 1995's *Bring in 'da Noise, Bring in 'da Funk* was a riotous celebration of the black experience in America, using hip-hop beats, spoken word (with slam poetry texts by Reg E. Gaines), and much music and dance. And what dance it was.

Noise/Funk was, first and foremost, a tap show, the dancing illustrating the many chapters of African-American life. A number on a slave ship, with dancers clinking chains and neck irons stood out, as did the *piece de resistance*, "Taxi," a pulsating tap dance about four young black men (a hip-hopper, student, businessman, and a man in uniform) trying to hail a cab. Over and over we hear the wheels screech away, and the men dance out their frustration. With *Noise/Funk*, Tony-winning choreographer and lead dancer Savion Glover cemented his reputation as the leading tap artist of his generation.

7. *SONG AND DANCE*

A fairly unique concept: Act One, song; Act Two, Dance. Originally titled *Tell Me On a Sunday*, Andrew Lloyd Webber set a two-act tale to variations on Paganini's A minor *Caprice* and wrote the first act as a song cycle for a young Englishwoman named Emma, who falls in and out of love with a guy called Joe. (We see and hear only Emma.) Act Two sets an entire ensemble dancing, acting out Joe's adventures in courtship, leading him finally to his Emma.

Despite the pedigree of Lloyd Webber and lyricist Richard Maltby, Jr. and the choreographic chops of ballet master Peter Martins, *Song and Dance* never really added up to anything other than a novelty concoction for two performers, Emma in Act One and Joe in Act Two.

8. *RIVERDANCE*

What began as a brief dance interlude at the 1994 Eurovision Song Contest has become an unparalleled worldwide dance phenomenon. Michael Flatley and Bill Whelan's space-filler has exploded into a gargantuan evening of song and dance and a stirring tribute to the power of Celtic myth.

Riverdance, as conceived by composer/lyricist

Whelan and principal dancer and choreographer Flatley, became an immediate sensation in Dublin, soon playing to capacity crowds in London and eventually all over the world. The show had played limited engagements in New York before, but finally hit Broadway in 2000, minus Flatley, who left the show prior to its London opening due to creative differences.

9. *MOVIN' OUT*

Twenty-four Billy Joel songs from several of his hit albums were cobbled together in an attempt to create a narrative about friendships over time. A large corps of dancers was put through its paces dancing not to pre-recorded Joel tracks, but by a pit band featuring a Billy Joel sound-alike, Michael Cavanaugh.

Director-choreographer Twyla Tharp unfortunately shaped the material literally (Sergeant O' Leary walking the beat, Brenda & Eddie still going steady, etc.), and without an original score, the weak material overshadowed the strength of the dancing. The show opened strongly, however, in October 2002.

10. *FOSSE*

1999 saw this snappy revue come to Broadway as one of the last gasps of Canadian production company Livent. *Fosse* was a collection of well-executed numbers originally created by the late, great Bob Fosse, focusing on all the media in which he worked—film, television, nightclubs, and, of course, Broadway. As a retrospective, it was splendid, but as a new musical, it was less well regarded (and often compared with *Dancin'*), and, like *Contact*, was a dance show which won a Best Musical Tony in an otherwise weak year.

Hard to Be a Diva
10 Outrageous Offstage Moments

They say there's a light for every broken heart on Broadway. What they don't tell you is there's a "diva fit" for every broken light on Broadway. Here are ten outrageous moments of offstage antics, weirdness, and just plain diva-hood.

1. ***RED, HOT AND BLUE* (1936)**

Red, Hot and Blue was a deliberate attempt to cash in on the success of *Anything Goes*: same librettists (Lindsay and Crouse), same composer-lyricist (Cole Porter), and same leading lady (Ethel Merman). New to this production: Bob Hope, Jimmy Durante, and a laughably egomaniacal billing war.

Durante and Hope came aboard after William Gaxton walked, allegedly after hearing Merman talk about how *huge* her part was compared to *everybody else's*. Then the egos really took over. Durante and Merman's people apparently thought each deserved top billing, and no compromise could be reached to suit the stars. The end result still gets a chuckle from the show freak: Cross-billing, Durante's name running from, say, eleven o'clock to five, and Merman's running from seven to one. (Hope's name ran inoffensively under both.) Not only does one think, "Wow, trained egos!" but also, "Hey, looks like the Scottish flag!"

2. *MISS SAIGON* (1991)

The pop-opera spectacle *Miss Saigon* was a monster hit in London, but as soon as producer Cameron Mackintosh announced his plans to bring the show, a Vietnam-era *Madama Butterfly*, to Broadway, chaos erupted.

Asian American playwright David Henry Hwang served notice with Equity, the actor's union, that he and a coalition of theater people objected to Mackintosh's intention of bringing Welsh actor Jonathan Pryce over from London to reprise his role of the Engineer, a Eurasian pimp. Hwang specifically objected to a pure European playing this Asian role with prosthetic eyelids when an Asian American actor could have played the role naturally.

As the press got wind of the controversy, Mackintosh countered by threatening to scrap the entire production, saying it was his to cast as he saw fit, and that Pryce (and Filipino actress Lea Salonga, also coming over from London) would open the show—or no one would.

Actor's Equity and Asian labor leaders chastised Hwang for his position, saying he was denying scores of Asian performers future employment opportunities. Ultimately, Hwang dropped his grievances, Pryce opened the role on Broadway (and won a Tony), and Mackintosh made good on his promise to hire Asian American performers to replace Pryce in the role of The Engineer.

3. *NINE* (1982)

The original Broadway production of *Nine* was a bliss-ful exercise in many different musical theater styles. One of the highlights of the show was Anita Morris's performance as Carla, the larger-than-life mistress of the musical's lead, Guido (Raul Julia). Clad in a see-through black jumpsuit, she seduces Guido over the phone in the fabulous "A Call From The Vatican." *Hello*, Tony Awards!

Except for the inevitable brouhaha. CBS-TV execu-tives pulled the plug on Morris performing her number at the last moment, saying the idea of a grown woman seducing a grown man was too adult for broadcast. So, the number they chose to broadcast instead was "Ti Voglio Bene (Be Italian)," a memory number with Young Guido and his chums being taught the ways of *amore* by the local whore, Saraghina (Kathi Moss). So . . . hot redhead on the phone? Sorry, no. Colorful whore with a group of young boys? Why, sure! "A vast wasteland," indeed.

4. *1776* (1969)

1776 was 1969's big musical hit, and actor William Daniels' performance as John Adams, simultaneously charming and frustrating, was the year's finest musical performance. So fine, in fact, that he refused to play in the same league with his co-stars come Tony time.

Since *1776* was a show with a huge male ensemble cast, no single performer was given star billing with his name above the show's title. So when the Tony award nominations were announced, Daniels was listed in the Featured (supporting) category. Daniels objected, rightly stating that his was a lead performance, and requested that the committee remove his name from the Featured category. The Tony committee acquiesced, and the Featured Actor Tony went to Ron Holgate, also from *1776*. Holgate had one show-stopping number and literally about half the stage time Daniels had. Daniels was not nominated in the Lead Actor category.

5. *STARLIGHT EXPRESS* (1987)

Andrew Lloyd Webber and Richard Stilgoe's *Starlight Express* is a musical bedtime story: a tale about trains competing in a race, ultimately won by Rusty, the old steam engine, who embraces the Starlight Express, the God figure of the show.

A decidedly subpar offering from Lloyd Webber, *Starlight Express* tells its rail tale with its actors, on skates, playing the trains. For Broadway, set designer John Napier created a staggering travelogue-of-America set, complete with a mammoth mechanized bridge. Tony voters were less than staggered, though, and nominated Napier's clever *Starlight* costumes but not his set.

On the night of the Awards, Napier indeed won for his costumes, and a minute later, he won for his brilliant set for *Les Miserables*. He made his thanks to his staff, and then he wondered aloud why his *Starlight* set wasn't nominated. Seventeen people in the Mark Hellinger Theater applauded, then Napier stated he'd swap his Tony "to have been in the room," backhanding the Nominating Committee. He then quickly added, "You know? Thanks," then hit the road, leaving a stunned, silent audience to wonder what had happened. And . . . let's go to commercial. (No hard feelings; Napier won again in 1995, for yet another massive, two-level Lloyd Webber set, *Sunset Blvd.*)

6. *VICTOR/VICTORIA* (1996)

When Blake Edwards and his wife, Julie Andrews, decided to bring their film musical, *Victor/Victoria*, to Broadway, the gossip immediately began. When rumors of creative trouble on the production started to surface, the gossip started again. And when the 1996 Tony nominations were announced, the gossip went into overdrive.

Victor/Victoria, the story of a woman pretending to be a female impersonator, was a superb film musical, expertly weaving its storybook-like Parisian musical comedy with sex-farce machinations. Edwards reportedly had trouble successfully adapting his movie for the stage, and the Leslie Bricusse tunes augmenting the late Henry Mancini's movie songs were not well integrated.

Reviews, except those for Andrews, were bad, and hers was the only Tony nomination the show received. On May 8, 1996, she addressed the audience at the Marquis Theater, after her curtain call, to announce that she was refusing the nomination, preferring to "stand with the egregiously overlooked," referring to the cast and authors. The Nominating Committee did not honor Andrews' request, and Tony host Nathan Lane twitted her mercilessly on the awards broadcast.

7. *SENATOR JOE* (1989)

Producer Adela Holzer had a strange and not-too-successful track record on Broadway; her taste in projects always veered toward the cockeyed. Unfortunately, her business acumen tended to stray from the path as well. Her last Broadway stint was on *Senator Joe*.

By all accounts, *Senator Joe* was going to be a routinely bad rock opera about everyone's favorite Commie-hunter, Joe McCarthy. Mostly the work of frequent Holzer confederate Tom O' Horgan, it began its preview period on January 5, 1989, and shuttered forever just two days later. Holzer, jailed shortly after for financial irregularities, had a track record of shady financial schemes, including a recent immigration scam. Actress Tovah Feldshuh, however, puts it all in perspective: "Adela Holzer," she told online columnist Peter Filichia, "was very good to her actors."

8. *SUBWAYS ARE FOR SLEEPING* (1961)

After Brooks Atkinson retired from the *New York Times*, people should have seen this one coming. Producer David Merrick, the "Abominable Showman" his ownself, played a publicity prank for his musical *Subways Are for Sleeping* that still gets a chuckle and a head shake today.

Merrick found seven men whose names matched the names of the drama critics of the seven daily New York papers. He took them to dinner and the show, they all had a lovely time, and he quoted their "rave reviews" in an ad shortly after. The fact that Merrick printed their pictures next to the names should have tipped off the ad editors, but the ad inexplicably slipped through to the morning edition of the January 4 *Herald Tribune*. There is no more *Subways Are for Sleeping*. There is no more *Herald Tribune*. 'Nuff said.

9. *IT AIN'T NOTHIN' BUT THE BLUES* (1999)

Another potential Tony Award brouhaha, which was actually more of a tempest in a teacup. The high-spirited (but, ultimately, rather toothless) blues revue, *It Ain't Nothin' But the Blues*, racked up a precious Best Musical Tony nomination in 1999, guaranteeing the show a performance spot on the TV broadcast. Right? Wrong. Cut to two hours of airtime by CBS, the Tony broadcast was running behind, and the number from *Blues* was axed. Following the ceremony, the myriad producers of the musical complained to the press, thereby guaranteeing the show more publicity than it ever would have received if the show had been seen on the Tonys. As a consolation prize, CBS booked the show on "Late Night With David Letterman," but *Blues* closed shortly after anyway.

10. *YOUR OWN THING* (1968)

Your Own Thing was a popular and critical hit off-Broadway during the 1967–68 season. By coincidence, it was also one of the worst years ever for Broadway musicals. When *Your Own Thing* won the Drama Critics Award, producer Zev Bufman lobbied to get *Your Own Thing* considered for Tony award eligibility, hoping to expand the horizons and blur the lines between Broadway and off-Broadway.

Predictably, Broadway producers stamped, and hissed, and shouted Bufman down, preferring instead to cling to shows like the eventual winner, *Hallelujah, Baby!* (Remember it? Well, *do* you?) This argument is raised every generation or so when off-Broadway producers see a chance to increase the profile of their own shows by invoking the "lack of quality new shows on Broadway" rant.

All Things Bright and Beautiful
10 Musicals about the Animal Kingdom

Musicals about animals are a risky proposition. Movies make animals walk and talk with ease, while on the stage, a certain stylization is called for. These ten shows took the plunge anyway.

1. *THE LION KING*

A Broadway stage version of Disney's animated hit film "The Lion King" seemed like a slam dunk; still, few would have expected the finished product to be quite this successful. Tim Rice, Hans Zimmer, and Elton John's movie score was agreeably padded for the stage, but the true star of the evening (and perhaps the decade) was director and costume designer Julie Taymor, who, in tandem with her fellow designers, conjured up image after unbelievable image of the animal kingdom. A true triumph of both bread and circuses, *The Lion King* looks to be one of Broadway's evergreen titles.

2. *CATS*

T. S. Eliot's *Old Possum's Book of Practical Cats* was set to music by Andrew Lloyd Webber as far back as 1977; did I hear someone say international phenomenon? A marketing bonanza from a musical of people playing kitties all evening? Well, director Trevor Nunn (who originally imagined the show being played by "five talented performers") and his cohorts worked their typical '80s Brit-magic. With John Napier's spectacular set, transforming the theater into a human-scaled cat's junkyard, and ingenious props and costumes to support Eliot's irresistible verses and Lloyd Webber's superbly theatrical music, *Cats* became a leviathan, the longest-running musical in both London and Broadway history.

3. *MOBY DICK*

Another London smash, *Moby Dick* was a radical re-imagining of Melville's classic tale. While retaining the story of the obsessed Captain Ahab and the *Pequod*'s quest for the great white whale proper, the show's authors framed it with a girls' school "performance" of *Moby Dick* for Parents' Weekend. Producer Cameron Mackintosh picked up the small-scale pop-rock show and took it to a prize-winning run in the West End, the production emphasizing creative staging and a youthful cast. The show has had little success in the States, offering a delicious irony: A musicalization of one of the great American novels proved a hit in England but a flop in The United States.

4. *THE YEARLING*

Marjorie Kinnan Rawlings' great novel of innocence lost was adapted for the stage in 1965, but lasted only three performances. To its credit, the yearling fawn in question was "played" by a real deer onstage, rather than an actor in a deer suit. The show, from a very bleak source to begin with, did not shy away from its depressing underpinnings and was not a success, but the score, by Michael Leonard and Herbert Martin, has its supporters.

5. *HONK!*

This version of Hans Christian Andersen's "Ugly Duckling" was originally produced regionally in England,

Marriott Theater

The cast of *Honk!*, a musical version of Hans Christian
Andersen's *Ugly Duckling*, at the Marriott Theater in Lincolnshire,
Illinois. Chicago actor Paul Slade Smith (top row, center)
is the honker in question.

and has found a life in regional productions around the United States as well. Once again, the animals are given human qualities, the bad Cat being a slick hustler, Grace the beautiful duck being a prissy pageant-queen type. But the spin put on Andersen's tale is quite funny and charming (Mother Ida, fearing her Ugly is really a turkey and looking him in the eye and saying "Butterball"), and the score by George Stiles and Anthony Drew works for both child and adults.

6. *EVERYTHING'S DUCKY*

The same tale again, this time adapted by Americans Henry Krieger, Bill Russell, and Jeffrey Hatcher, and the ugly duckling in question is a girl, Serena. She's also adopted, it turns out, and there's no unconditional love forthcoming from her mama at all. Unlike *Honk!*, this version is not a family-friendly version of the story, as the evil coyotes run a strip club, and Serena becomes a bitchy supermodel. She believes in herself, however, and that's the upshot of this tongue-in-cheek, adult version of the classic tale.

7. *SEUSSICAL, THE MUSICAL*

Lynn Ahrens and Stephen Flaherty's ultimately unsatisfying musical setting of stories by the late, great Dr. Seuss opened in 2000, after a year of development. The Cat in the Hat (played on Broadway by the too-edgy David Shiner) was to unify the evening, but the tales of Horton the Elephant, lazy Mayzie and her egg, the Whos, and many, many others were too dissimilar to unify into a musical. The songs, while professional, didn't possess the necessary Seussian sense of wonder, and the Cat was a strange choice to guide the evening—iconic, yes, but a bad kitty nonetheless. The

show has been radically rethought and redesigned for
its touring production.

8. *a YEar WITH FROG anD TOaD*

The popular series of children's books by Arnold Lobel
were musicalized in 2002 by the Reale brothers, Willie
and Robert, in Minneapolis, then off-Broadway. The
sweetness of the Lobel books transferred well to the
stage, and the musical transferred to Broadway in the
spring of 2003, where it was out of place among the
bigger, brassier shows. Jay Goede and Mark Linn-
Baker were the lighthearted Frog and the phlegmatic
Toad. Set designer Adrianne Lobel is the daughter of
author Arnold.

9. *THE WIND IN THE WILLOWS*

Kenneth Grahame's immortal children's novel about
Mr. Toad and the denizens of the Wild Woods has been
musicalized many times, both for stage and film. The
Broadway version played only four performances in
1985, yet was nominated for book and score Tonys due
to weak competition. This version, the work of William
Perry, Roger McGough, and Jane Iredale, made a mistake familiar to many "family" musicals—namely, ig-
noring subtextual elements intended for adult readers
to interpret for their children. This *Wind* is most notable
for its stellar cast of starts-to-be, including Tony winner
Scott Waara, Nora Mae Lyng, David Carroll, and a
young Nathan Lane as Toad.

10. *SHINBONE aLLEY*

New York *Sun* columnist Don Marquis wrote a series of
columns about archy the cockroach, and his cat friend
mehitabel, starting in 1916. In 1957, archy (lower case

because he typed his poems but couldn't operate the shift key) and mehitabel and their animal friends were immortalized on Broadway in *Shinbone Alley*. Broadway's first racially integrated cast featured the amazing Eartha Kitt as the indomitable mehitabel, and the late Eddie Bracken as her steadfast archy. Mel Brooks, Joe Darion, and George Kleinsinger adapted Marquis' verse for the stage as well as for concert presentation and an animated film.

Let's Do It

10 Musicals about S-E-X

Here, for your lascivious, exhibitionist pleasure, are ten musicals which address the oldest pleasure there is. Enjoy, sickos.

1. ***A LITTLE NIGHT MUSIC***

This magnificent musical adaptation of Ingmar Bergmann's film *Smiles of a Summer Night* concerns a legendary actress/courtesan, Desirée Armfeldt, and the amorous encounters of her former lover, his family, and another middle-aged couple on a Swedish country estate. All and sundry, guests and servants, pair off under the watchful summer night, which smiles on the young, the old, and the foolish. Stephen Sondheim, in peak form, wrote the score almost completely in variants of waltz time, including the classic nocturne "Send in the Clowns." Nineteen-seventy-two's Tony winner is universally regarded as a tasteful classic.

2. ***OUT OF THIS WORLD***

Cole Porter, who for so long masked his risqué lyrics due to censorship battles, finally had a chance to write about the great game in this 1950 musical. Unfortunately, while the score was great, and the sets were fantastic, the book was not up to the level of either.

Out of This World is a musical version of the Amphytrion saga, in which Jupiter disguises himself as a mortal general and leaves Olympus, in order to sleep with the general's wife. The score is typically excellent, but the book, which was written by Reginald Lawrence and Dwight Taylor, suffered in comparison to Porter's great score (which *still* got snipped by Boston bluenoses), and the show lasted only 157 performances.

3. *THE BEST LITTLE WHOREHOUSE IN TEXAS*

This show, despite its title, is actually less about sex than it is about tradition and the media. A tall Texas tale based on the real-life Chicken Ranch (where clients could barter for favors), under the auspices of Madam Mona and the good-natured, pragmatic local sheriff, the show originally inspired some controversy because of that title.

But in spite of the obvious possibilities for vulgarity, *Whorehouse* told its story with good taste, thanks mainly to a no-nonsense book by Larry L. King and Peter Masterson, and the superb work of director-choreographer-Texan Tommy Tune, only veering into Cartoonland when examining the motives of a holier-than-thou TV host intent on shutting down the beloved Ranch.

4. *NINE*

Another Tommy Tune stylistic exercise, 1981's Best Musical Tony winner is an erotic adaptation of Fellini's classic film *8½ (Otto e Mezzo)*. Like Fellini's film, it concerns a selfish, blocked film director in crisis with the women in his life: wife, mistress, protegeé, boss, etc. He is helped by his younger self to come to grips with his immaturity and to finally devote himself to one woman.

Also similarly to Fellini, the story was told mainly in black and white, Tune's fantastic staging set against Lawrence Miller's stark, white-tiled spa set and glorious black costumes by William Ivey Long. A very clever score by Maury Yeston was the capper to this sexy, stylish musical.

5. *scandal*

Broadway in the mid-1980s was a cold, cold place for musicals, and one reason was because Michael Bennett, the best director and choreographer of his generation, was largely dormant. Trade publications buzzed with rumors of Bennett's new musical, *Scandal*. Unfortunately, Bennett's great musical was not to be.

Scandal was written by pop songwriter Jimmy Webb and television writer Treva Silverman. The story of a married woman's search for self through sexual discovery, *Scandal* was assumed to have been Bennett's masterpiece, but a capricious (and, unfortunately, drug-troubled) Bennett prematurely pulled the plug on *Scandal*, for reasons which remain largely unknown. Many insiders speculate that Bennett's encroaching illness, which, of course, turned out to be AIDS, was the main reason. But all who witnessed Bennett's preproduction work on *Scandal* weep for what might have been.

6. *OH! CALCUTTA!*

Chances are if you said "sex musical" to someone on the street, they'd either keep walking, or they'd answer *Oh! Calcutta!* And so it is that *Oh! Calcutta!* (whose title is a bastardization of the French for "nice ass, honey") became part of the popular lexicon by being America's best-known nudie musical. The show, a fairly insubstantial trifle, was a record long-running song-sketch-dance revue, all about sex, sex, and more sex. Leering doctor-and-nurse sketches, trippy expressionistic dances, and dirty songs abounded, all kept afloat by tourist money. Choreographer Margo Sappington and writer and critic Kenneth Tynan were the driving forces behind *Oh! Calcutta!*, which, despite its long, long run, was always treated like Broadway's red-headed stepchild.

7. *I LOVE MY WIFE*

A funny, extremely tuneful farce based on a French comedy (of course) about wife-swapping, drug use, and other '70s taboos. Another example of Broadway audiences experiencing a vicarious thrill, *I Love My Wife* was a surprisingly cheerful and moral show.

We follow two couples, one of which is slightly wilder and "with it," and their good friends, who are more reserved, as they tensely dive into the forbidden fruits of you-know-what and you-know-which. The Cy Coleman-Michael Stewart score, featuring the topical "Married Couple Seeks Married Couple" and "Everybody Today is Turning On," plus the show-stopping "Hey There, Good Times," was the evening's highlight.

8. *THE FIG LEAVES ARE FALLING*

In a 1969 flop for those who think young, a mild-mannered college professor straight out of a Jean Kerr play decides to up and ditch his wife and family for a sweet young thing. The wife, instead of boo-hooing, fights back and, since she's played by Dorothy Loudon, she wins.

A supposedly naughty show which actually held no

surprises at all—everyone pretty much saw right through this one—sniggered at its characters where a better musical might have sympathized with them. The book and lyrics were by Allan "Hello Muddah, Hello Fadduh" Sherman, and while his parody lyrics are clever, they obviously can't supply enough material for a whole book musical.

9. *DEBBIE DOES DALLAS*

This off-Broadway musical from 2002 was based on the, uh, classic 1977 porn film. In these situations, plot is very important, so here goes: Debbie wants to be a professional cheerleader and is willing to make her dreams come true. Despite an earnest performance by Sherie Renee Scott in the title role, and the presence of a whole lot of music, *Debbie Does Dallas* failed.

Why, do you suppose? Well, maybe because stupid retro musicals are bad enough, but when you make one out of a hardcore porn film, you've obviously got nothing to hang your satire on. What are you going to do, show us? Of course not. It's a cynical way to create a musical, and was rewarded in kind.

10. *HELLO AGAIN*

Sex gets experimental in composer-lyricist Michael John LaChiusa's take on Schnitzler's *La Ronde*. LaChiusa's conceit was to take the bones of Schnitzler's dirty little tale and transport it to the twentieth century. We see the stock characters ("The soldier," "The whore," "The nurse") jumping in and out of bed with each other while jumping back and forth between the decades. Again, graceful staging (by Graciela Daniele) served LaChiusa's writing well, saving what could well have been a dirty little nothing.

Oh, I Say!

10 Broadway Musicals Whose Titles Are Complete Sentences

Editors love complete sentences; they make for easy editing and fun reading. Broadway producers don't usually like musicals with long titles; they're hard to grasp while walking down the street. Here are ten musicals whose titles probably tested their producers' patience.

1. *YOU NEVER KNOW*

Cole Porter scored this charmer about a bon vivant German baron and his simple English valet who switch identities in the hothouse environment of a Paris hotel suite. Unwisely blown out of proportion (against the authors' wishes) to include a singing, dancing chorus prior to its Broadway engagement in 1938, it was a 78-performance flop. But luckily for all, this jewel box of a musical farce has, with some re-shaping, finally been scaled down to six characters in search of "At Long Last Love."

2. **SUBWAYS ARE FOR SLEEPING**

This Jule Styne–Betty Comden–Adolph Green tuner about the happy-go-lucky homeless (by choice!) denizens of New York City's subways seemed less than quaint even in 1961, and obviously its central conceit hasn't aged well. The most interesting thing about the show was the life-imitates-art episode in which New York's real homeless began interpreting the show's posters as an invitation to spend the night on the trains.

3. **I CAN GET IT FOR YOU WHOLESALE**

The incomparable Barbra Streisand shot to stardom as frumpy secretary Miss Marmelstein in this poison-pen love letter to the roguish antihero Harry Bogen (played by Elliot Gould), who was making a name in Manhattan's garment district at the expense of literally everything else in his life. While not overly charming, Harold Rome and Jerome Weidman's show was praised as being true to its rather cynical Seventh Avenue milieu.

4. **I DO! I DO!**

A novelty musical from the novel minds of Tom Jones and Harvey Schmidt, by way of playwright Jan de Hartog. His play *The Fourposter* was musicalized faithfully, as only two performers (originally the dream team of Mary Martin and Robert Preston) enacted fifty years as man and wife, the songs acting as scenes ("Love Isn't Everything" detailed two Blessed Events) or as commentary (the hit "My Cup Runneth Over").

5. **SHE LOVES ME**

A nearly perfect musical with a passionate following, this charming musical was adapted by Joseph Stein,

Jerry Bock, and Sheldon Harnick from Miklos Laszlo's play *Parfumerie,* which also served as source material for the films *The Shop Around the Corner* and *You've Got Mail.*

Tone is everything in the telling of the familiar tale of two co-workers who fall in love through anonymous correspondence, yet can't stand each other face-to-face. *She Loves Me* was the directorial debut of musical titan Harold Prince, and the three writers, with Prince producing, went on to create the classic *Fiddler on the Roof.*

6. *I LOVE MY WIFE*

Cy Coleman and Michael Stewart's swingin' '70s musical about, well, swingin'. Wordsmith Stewart had seen a sexy French boulevard farce loosely translated as *Come On Up To My Place, I'm Living With My Girlfriend* and became intrigued with the idea of musicalizing the at-the-time in-vogue hobby of wife-swapping.

The show hit Broadway, where the musicians were in full view onstage, and costumes were changed (and often discarded) in sight of the audience, adding to the anything-goes vibe of the evening. Coleman's score and director Gene Saks's relatively sensitive yet very funny handling of this potentially crude material helped carry *I Love My Wife* to an 857-performance run.

7. *DO I HEAR A WALTZ?*

Indeed you do, courtesy of Broadway's own Waltz King, Richard Rodgers. Stephen Sondheim was the lyricist and Arthur Laurents adapted his own play *The Time of the Cuckoo*, which had previously been filmed, with Katharine Hepburn, as *Summertime* in 1955.

Legendary squabbles between the collaborators

have soured many on this 1965 musical, dealing with a middle-aged woman who vacations in Venice and longs for romance. The air of vulnerability and longing inherent in the Hepburn film and Laurents's play were missing from the musicalization, which some saw as too representative of the oil-and-water Sondheim-Rodgers partnership.

8. *a Funny THING HaPPENED ON THE Way TO THE FORUM*

Prior to waltzing with Rodgers, Stephen Sondheim partied with Plautus, Titus Macchius Plautus to be specific, in this riotous Roman spoof from 1962. That the title sounds like the set-up to an old vaudeville gag is no coincidence: Librettists Larry Gelbart and Burt Shevelove conceived their show as a modern-day musical paean to the comedies of Plautus, finding in this Father of Comic Situation a corollary to the schtick-meisters and low comics of the zany days of burlesque. (Milton Berle, apparently not getting the point, reportedly passed on playing the lead because he thought it was "old schtick.")

9. *ON a CLEAR Day you can SEE FOREVER*

In 1965, Alan Jay Lerner teamed with the long-inactive composer Burton Lane for an unusual little musical about ESP and reincarnation. (Yep, it was the sixties, all right.) John Cullum played a flashy doctor treating a patient (the flighty yet adorable Barbara Harris) who believes she has been reincarnated.

Daisy Gamble (Harris) took the audience back with her to her previous existence in Regency England, giving Lerner a chance to indulge his expertise in *My Fair Lady*-like verbiage (and, incidentally, pad out the thin plot). A fine score, including the sensational "Cosy and Tosh" and "Come Back to Me," was nearly all that was salvaged from this 280-performance disappointment.

10. *LEAVE IT TO ME!*

Another Cole Porter show (1939), an adaptation of Sam and Bella Spewack's wacky spoof of Communism and geopolitical values *Clear All Wires. Leave It to Me!* is most fondly remembered today for Mary Martin's Broadway debut, wowing 'em as she stripped off her Raoul Pene DuBois fur to the strains of "My Heart Belongs to Daddy." Audiences of the time also enjoyed the vicarious pleasure of seeing a Nazi get the crap kicked out of him by the American Ambassador to Soviet Russia while Stalin pranced about the stage.

Monorail!
10 Musical Theater Spoofs

Think writing and performing a musical is hard? Try writing a *satire* of a musical. Then make it funny. Not as easy as it seems. Here are ten very funny musical spoofs from other arms of the pop-culture octopus.

1. *OH! STREETCAR!* ("A STREETCAR NAMED MARGE," THE SIMPSONS)

Conan O'Brien's "Monorail" episode is a riotously funny (hence the title of this chapter) take-off on *The Music Man*'s "Ya Got Trouble," but the prize for the best *Simpsons* musical spoof goes to *Oh! Streetcar!* Marge, feeling neglected, tries out for a community theater production of *Oh! Streetcar!*, a musical version of the Tennessee Williams classic. Guest actor Jon Lovitz scores big time as the musical's *auteur*, Llewellyn Sinclair, who routinely insults his charges while wearing a ridiculous muumuu.

Oh! Streetcar! takes off on *Les Misérables* (as the curtain rises on a revolving turntable featuring the Louisiana Superdome on one side and the Kowalski/Hubbell apartment building on the other) and other '80's spectacles (Marge flies through the air on wires, in the middle of a laser light show), and mercilessly skewers bad musical theater with awful forced rhymes ("Mardi Gras" with "party, hah") and just plain inappropriate writing. One song describes the innermost feelings of Blanche's paperboy, and the upbeat, doo-wacka finale "You Can Always Depend on the Kindness of Strangers," is pure gold.

2. *FINIAN'S RAINBOW, STARRING THE MAN FROM THE OFF-LICENCE* (MONTY PYTHON'S FLYING CIRCUS)

The Pythons were all academics who started on the stage, and their legendary sketch comedy show often satirized musical theater, usually British music-hall styles. But one sketch in Episode Nineteen, an interview with Mr. F. L. Dibley, tells us he is a filmmaker who has all his great ideas "stolen" before his movies get back from the developer. (The Interviewer: "Mr. Dibley, some people have drawn comparisons between your film *if,* which ends with a gun battle at a public school, and Mr. Lindsay Anderson's film *if*, which ends with a gun battle at a public school.")

Mr. Dibley's latest masterpiece is *Finian's Rainbow Starring the Man from the Off-Licence* (the English equivalent of a liquor store), and we see a film clip of *Python*'s Michael Palin in a dress, looking uncomfortable, trying to run from the screen, and, finally, doing a most unconvincing little dance. Dibley (Terry Jones) puts it bitterly: "a real failure that was. Ten seconds of solid boredom." Maybe, but hilarious nonetheless.

3. *H.M.S. YAKKO* (ANIMANIACS)

Animaniacs, the crazy, often side-splittingly funny Warner Bros. animated trio, were tended by writers with a great sense of the history that had made their postmodern, retro-hip look at the world of animated cartoons possible. To many, the greatest pleasure of *Animaniacs* was the use of a Carl Stalling–like orchestra of what seemed like thousands, playing zany musical cues at the drop of a hat (or, in the case of Yakko, Wakko, and Dot Warner, the drop of an anvil).

Often, their adventures were of a musical nature, and writer/director Paul Rugg created the episode *H.M.S. Yakko* as an unabashed homage to Gilbert and Sullivan, in particular the two "maritime" shows, *H.M.S. Pinafore* and *The Pirates of Penzance*. The Warners are merely riding a whale to the beach to relax (don't ask), but they run afoul of the evil pirate Captain Mel, who is so evil and inept that he has two peg legs. Included in the zaniness are song parodies of startling fidelity to spirit of the Messrs. Gilbert & Sullivan, the comic patter songs ("I Am the Very Model of a Cartoon Individual," Yakko sings) specifically.

4. *ELEPHANT! THE MUSICAL* (THE TALL GUY)

Also stepping out in finery borrowed from *Les Miserables* is Mel Smith's 1990 film *The Tall Guy*. It's the story of a luckless American actor (Jeff Goldblum) appearing as the very second banana in a West End revue. After his boss (Rowan Atkinson, a flinty Napoleon-type) fires him, he gets a job as the non-singing (because he's tone-deaf) lead in *Elephant! The Musical*, based, of course, on Bernard Pomerance's *The Elephant Man*. Bandied about by the director at the opening night party is a musical version of *Richard III*, with a tune called "(I've got a hunch) I'm going to be King."

A very funny send-up of the Brit-popera formula, *Elephant!* includes a soft-shoe danced by actors in elephant masks (which concludes with the ensemble yanking on their trunks), lyrics like "Here he comes, Mister Disgusting!," and a finale entitled "Somewhere Up in Heaven, There's an Angel With Big Ears," sung by a walk-to-the-footlights chorus as the Elephant Man's bed is raised to the heavens.

5. "ONCE MORE, WITH FEELING" (*BUFFY THE VAMPIRE SLAYER*)

Joss Whedon, the creator of TV's hugely successful *Buffy the Vampire Slayer*, penned the songs and script for this episode, *Buffy*'s contribution to the "musical mania" that swept through network TV in the early part of the new millennium.

Buffy the Vampire Slayer staked (sorry!) its ground by using the wolfsbane-and-ass-kicking travails of its heroes as metaphor for the fears and phobias of everyday lives of teenagers and young adults. The postmodern deconstruction of the show carried over into this episode, as the residents of Sunnyvale burst into song and dance for no good reason, Buffy's gang included. Turns out they are under the thumb of a song-and-dance demon (played to the hilt by three-time Tony winner Hinton Battle) who wants the populace to dance themselves to death until he can take his queen back to the underworld.

Whedon's songs, while containing several good lyrics, are not particularly distinguished musically, and no great step forward from the typical styles of middling Disney animated films. Still, the cast, all of whom can at least carry a tune, deserve points for trying.

6. "SOMEBODY HAS TO PLAY CLEOPATRA" (*THE DICK VAN DYKE SHOW*)

Perhaps the funniest half-hour in TV sitcom history, this episode of *The Dick Van Dyke Show* aired on December 26, 1962. The show's hero, Rob Petrie (Van Dyke) is a bit of a local celebrity in his quiet New Rochelle neighborhood, because he writes for *The Alan Brady Show*. This naturally brings out the "star" in everyone, and this dilemma reaches a head in the neighborhood's annual talent show.

Mrs. Billings, chairman of the variety show, manages to rope Rob in every year, ("Ohhh, Mr. Petrie! It's so eeeeeeeeeeeasy for you!" squeals the magnificent Eleanor Audley), so his plate is already full writing and directing the show. Then we get to the rehearsal in the Petrie home. After Laura (Mary Tyler Moore) wows 'em with her calypso number, "True, Mon, True," we get to the show's Cleopatra sketch. The Petrie's neighbor Millie is Cleopatra, while another neighbor, Harry Roberts (Bob Crane), is Marc Antony. He's so enthusiastic, he's turned his sweater into a toga and changed "I have arrived from Rome" to "I have a-Romed from Rive." Trouble is, Millie's husband Jerry objects to the passionate kiss the two share, and he dares Rob to put Laura in the sketch instead.

Rob bites, Laura kisses Harry, and Rob suggests they merely shake hands instead, ha-ha. Laura guesses the problem and withdraws, leaving only the mousy kindergarten teacher to play Cleopatra. And when her glasses come off and her hair comes down? Hel-looo, Nurse! It is at this time, as Antony and Cleo kiss *again*, that Harry's good wife walks in, sees him, and walks out the door, yelling at him to come home. After an off-screen shouting match, Crane sticks his head in and sheepishly offers one of the greatest punch lines ever: "One of the kids is sick."

7.   *I'M TAKING MY OWN HEAD, SCREWING IT ON RIGHT AND NO GUY'S GONNA TELL ME IT AIN'T!* (SCTV TELEVISION NETWORK)

Before there was a Tony for Andrea Martin (for 1992's *My Favorite Year*), there was *SCTV* in Canada. It was on this great sketch comedy series, with fellow cast members, John Candy, Catherine O'Hara, Joe Flaherty, Rick Moranis, and Martin Short, that some of the greatest characters in TV history, including Libby Wolfson, were born.

Libby Wolfson was Martin's "Eighties woman" creation, a clueless, self-empowerment-spouting host of her own SCTV gab-show, *You!*. What made the concept work was that Wolfson was really just a mess of insecurities ("I would kill to be anorexic for one week," she once told a guest on her show) who needed constant on-screen validation from her best friend, Sue Bopper-Simpson (Catherine O'Hara).

Together, Wolfson and Simpson created *I'm Taking My Own Head, Screwing it on Right, and No Guy's Gonna Tell Me It Ain't. Head* was a send-up of the late-seventies/early eighties "lib" shows popularized by Nancy Ford and Gretchen Cryer, the most obvious target being their "find myself" show *I'm Getting My Act Together and Taking it On the Road*. With the pliable Seth Dick III as the show's all-purpose Man, *Head* played one pathetic performance and closed. Further evidence of the multi-level brilliance of *SCTV*: The SCTV Network's prickly social critic, Bill Needle (Dave Thomas), is busted down to theater critic, and proceeds to take Wolfson's show apart on his new TV show, "Theater Beat."

8. **A MASKED BALL (*THE ADVENTURE OF SHERLOCK HOLMES' SMARTER BROTHER*)**

Film star Gene Wilder made his directorial debut with *The Adventure of Sherlock Holmes' Smarter Brother*, a film that, with its obvious period trappings, cheerful vulgarity, and primitive craftsmanship, seems directly influenced by that '70's camp-film *auteur*, Wilder's good friend and colleague Mel Brooks.

Basically the title says it all, as the great detective hands one off to his brother, Sigerson Holmes (Wilder), to solve. It involves stolen letters and a performance of the opera *A Masked Ball*, directed by and starring the evil Gambetti (Dom DeLuise), in league with Professor Moriarity (Leo McKern). It is at this opening-night performance that Sigerson Holmes (with an assist from his dumber brother) solves the case and saves the day and the Empire.

The "Masked Ball" in the movie bears no relation to Verdi's comic masterpiece; rather, it sounds like *Le Nozze di Figaro* plus Monty Python divided by P.D.Q. Bach. Madeline Kahn is hilarious as a diva in danger, singing lines like "Stop that, you're such a tickle-tease/ You know I'm super-passionate."

9. RED, WHITE, AND BLAINE! (*WAITING FOR GUFFMAN*)

Christopher Guest's documentary-style parody of community theater rates high on the showbiz "in-joke-o-meter" for its funny, often brutal takeoff on community theater types presenting a pageant in their hometown of Blaine, Missouri (the "Stool Capital of the World").

The good people of Blaine are put through their paces by the indefatigable Corky St. Clair, a failed drama queen with gumption enough for two Marjorie Main movies. His show, *Red, White, and Blaine!*, sounds like pretty much any amateur musical you'd care to name, with one ballad, "A Penny For Your Thoughts," that could stand outside a parody film like this. The condescending tone of much of the movie is made palatable by the gold-standard cast that Guest assembled: Eugene Levy, Fred Willard, Catherine O'Hara, and Parker Posey as four of the stalwarts, with cameos by Paul Benedict, David Cross, and Paul Dooley adding to the fun.

10. JEEPERS CREEPERS SEMI-STAR (*MR. SHOW*)

Television's last great sketch-comedy show was the late, lamented *Mr. Show* from HBO, and one reason for the show's greatness was the fearlessness of their parodies. The first season gave audiences "Joke, the Musical," a very funny community-therater-level musicalization of the joke about the traveling salesman and the three holes in the barn wall. *Jeepers Creepers Semi-Star* earns them the nod here, though.

As you could probably guess, it's a parody of *Jesus Christ Superstar*, and an almost spot-on parody at that. It's a scrupulously faithful homage to Norman Jewison's film version of *Superstar*, with the "troupe" piling out of a school bus and dancing in the desert somewhere, as Mr. and Mrs. Creepers sing ersatz Rice-Lloyd Webber about their apathetic, not-quite-perfect son Jeepers.

Historical News Is Being Made

10 Innovative Musicals

The musical theater is an expanding, ever-changing art form, and its progress through the decades is fun to chart. These ten musicals gave us something new.

1. *SHOW BOAT* (1927)

The granddaddy of them all, the first true musical play, *Show Boat*, adapted from Edna Ferber's novel, was the first Broadway musical entertainment to combine the musical lushness and grandiose trappings of old-school operetta with new, uncompromising storytelling techniques—the playlet *The Parson's Bride* on the boat, for instance, underscoring the love and family relationships being shaped at the same time in real life.

Jerome Kern's music and Oscar Hammerstein's book and lyrics are legendary now, but how amazing it must have been to see, as the curtain rose, colored performers, not happy blackfaced minstrels but dockworkers bent over their hay bales, singing "Niggers all work on de Missisippi,/Niggers all work while de white folks play." An uncompromising look at race, miscegenation, and even gambling, *Show Boat* presented its themes and characters with astounding freshness.

2. *ALLEGRO* (1947)

Richard Rodgers and Oscar Hammerstein II, the vanguard of musical storytelling, gave us *Allegro* in 1947, and in doing so, gave us the first true "concept musical"—a show about *how* it was about, rather than *what* it was about. A bare stage, with props and scenery rolled on and off as needed, with even a Greek chorus to tell the tale.

But what tale is being told? Is it just the tale of small-town doctor Joe, who moves away from the tiny hamlet that reared him, to the big city where he flourishes financially but dries up spiritually? Not exactly. Rodgers, Hammerstein, and director/choreographer Agnes de Mille played not only with music, lyrics, and dance, but also with time and space. For the first time, characters were seen inhabiting space they couldn't have possibly have existed in, either as real characters or dream figures. The hero's long-dead mother appears on stage to guide him through the play's finale, and a Greek chorus appears in the hospital delivery room to announce his birth. *Allegro* is perhaps not up to par with other R & H masterpieces, but it's a most valuable show in the evolution of the form.

3. *NO STRINGS* (1962)

Following the death of his longtime collaborator, Oscar Hammerstein, Richard Rodgers chose to write his own lyrics for his next show, *No Strings*, in 1962. No strings, indeed: The pit band had no stringed instruments and often no pit. Director Joe Layton's concept involved many of the musicians wandering into the action, which was deliberately stylized and artificially staged, often on a bare stage with lights clearly visible and aimed by hand for effect, with ensemble members forming *tableaux* to comment on foreground action.

The plot, concerning the relationship between a black fashion model and a white American writer bumming around Paris, also echoes the title: Theirs is a romance with no strings attached or so each would like to think. This interracial love relationship was considerably risky for 1962 but skillfully put forth with little fanfare. It helps if she's a world-class fashion model played by Diahann Carroll.

4. *COMPANY* (1970)

"New York City—NOW." Those words, place and time, set the tone perfectly for *Company*, Stephen Sondheim and George Furth's landmark musical meditation on marriage, friendship, and commitment. Furth's ideas for several one-act plays were assembled by director Harold Prince into a plotless musical, with a score by Sondheim, that moved, looked, and sounded like no musical ever had. Furth's script places the action in scrambled time and place, with the whole play really taking place in a split second, in a kind of theatrical limbo.

Choreographer Michael Bennett made the company of fourteen actors move by using their personal strengths (like watching the New Rochelle PTA, as some have observed) to real dramatic effect. Prince put them through their paces on Boris Aronson's remarkable abstract, steel-and-glass set, complete with working elevators, often isolating the players in stage spaces as if each couple were alone together in the big

Playbill/Meghan Falica

Company was Stephen Sondheim and George Furth's landmark musical dissection of marriage and commitment. This musical rewrote many of the rules for modern musical storytelling.

city. Sondheim's score was rightly hailed as a blistering examination of nerves and neuroses, pulsating to the busy-signal, traffic-jam rhythms of the city, with everyone proclaiming their fidelity to their friend Robert, their "Bobby Baby, Bobby Bubi," as if their very survival depended on him.

5. *PAL JOEY* (1940)

John O' Hara's *New Yorker* series of letters from his "pal Joey" served as the inspiration for Rodgers and Hart's classic 1940 musical, the first musical with a rat for a hero. In fact, just about everyone in this spiked gimlet of a show is pretty rotten. Up and down the social scale, the lives examined are all unfulfilled, and the unblinking, straightforward way these lives are examined was bracingly new to the musical theater.

Our pal Joey is a charismatic louse with a little bit of song-and-dance talent; his goal in life is to own his own nightclub ("Chez Joey"—that's *classy*) in Chicago. On his way up, he meets a sweet young kid of whom he takes advantage, and a rich older broad who takes advantage of him (who both agree in song that he's no damn good). Never had characters sounded and acted quite as they do in *Pal Joey*, neither sentimental nor completely evil either. Chicago's seedy underbelly was deftly examined by Rodgers and Hart (and by no-nonsense director George Abbott), and critics, even if they found the show distasteful, got the message: Musical theater was growing up.

6. *LOVE LIFE* (1948)

The prodigiously gifted composer Kurt Weill seemed to make musical theater history as he went along, from his work with Bertolt Brecht in their native Germany culminating in class-conscious masterpieces like *The Threepenny Opera*, to his work in his adopted United States, where he created political *zeitopers* like *Knickerbocker Holiday* and *Johnny Johnson*. *Love Life*, his 1948 collaboration with the great Alan Jay Lerner, was another step forward in the life of the American musical.

Love Life told the story of the American family, examining love, marriage, children, economics, and the social structure. The Coopers, a nuclear family, are seen through 150-plus years of Americana, yet they don't age. Interspersed with scenes from each time period are intercalary "vaudeville" numbers which provide commentary on the book scenes and give them depth, such as when the harried wife and mother is sawed in two by a magician, or in Michael Kidd's the-title-says-it-all ballet, "Punch and Judy Get a Divorce."

7. *SHUFFLE ALONG* (1921)

The legendary songwriting team of Eubie Blake and Noble Sissle reached their peak in 1921 with *Shuffle Along*, often credited as the first black musical. It was truly the first musical written, directed, and performed by blacks, but its significance reaches farther than that. *Shuffle Along* can honestly share the credit for launching an entire cultural movement.

Blake and Sissle met Flournoy Miller and Aubrey Lyles at a benefit for the NAACP in 1920. The four decided to create their own musical comedy, and the result was *Shuffle Along*, which broke many barriers. By showing the performers, and the characters they played, as real human beings (real in a musical-comedy sense, anyway), instead of servile clowns or objects of cartoonish lust, and by making a hit show while doing so, *Shuffle Along* was a touchstone for the advancement of African American art and culture. The Harlem Renaissance, that glorious era of creativity, began at the same time that *Shuffle Along* toured America. Producer Florenz Ziegfeld also hired many of the Negro performers to teach dance steps to his chorus girls, to lend them an air of authenticity.

The show itself is best described, as pianist Dick Hyman has said, as a "musical melange." Many song styles are present—the hit "Love Will Find a Way" hinting at Jerome Kern, as well as the two-step classic "I'm Just Wild About Harry," which was actually written as a waltz!

8.   *A CHORUS LINE* (1975)

A Chorus Line is the show that gave the anonymous dancers of the ensemble a forum to be heard, and the way director-choreographer Michael Bennett conceived and executed the show is the stuff of theatrical legend. *A Chorus Line* stands as the apotheosis of the showbiz musical, a show so tightly coordinated that its elements are almost diminished by examining them separately.

Michael Bennett loved dancers, and in now-legendary taped bull sessions, his dancers opened their souls to him and to each other. Whose idea it was to take these confessional tapes and fashion a musical from them is much debated, but Bennett had the clout, and the Public Theater's Joseph Papp had the checks, to allow Bennett to "workshop" his budding dance musical away from prying eyes. Co-librettists James Kirkwood and Nicholas Dante formed much of *A Chorus Line*'s confessional nature out of actual monologues from the tapes (including Dante's own drag-queen speech, given to the character Paul). The score, by Marvin Hamlisch and Edward Kleban, is a superb amalgam of showbiz cliches and pure emotion.

But the true hero of the creation of *A Chorus Line* is Michael Bennett. Bennett, the great *auteur* of seventies musicals who learned at the feet of the seventies' *other* genius director, Harold Prince, so precisely focused the content of *A Chorus Line* in workshop and rehearsal that its theme—the idea of an audience learning something about dancers as they auditioned for a Broadway show—was immediately clear to all who saw it. Not only a triumph of the "workshop" system and a masterpiece of collaboration, *A Chorus Line* also finally serves as a potent metaphor for anyone who has ever "put themselves on the line"—whether it be at work, in love, or with family.

q. *OKLAHOMA!* (1943)

If their careers were a graph, Richard Rodgers and Oscar Hammerstein II would inevitably have met with the monolithic *Oklahoma!* Think about it—the heretofore witty, sophisiticated tunesmith Rodgers, famous for *Pal Joey* and "Manhattan," writing with Oscar Hammerstein II, he of the frou-frou trappings of *Show Boat* and *The Desert Song* (or, as one wag labeled their collaboration, "smart meets heart"). We'll see.

But wait. They're writing a *western* musical? With no cowboy ballads? No big hoedowns? No dancing girlies? Their musical play, as their producers, the Theater Guild, called it, based on Lynn Riggs' play *Green Grow the Lilacs*, *Oklahoma!* broke most of the ground rules of musical theater writing that these two gentlemen had already set down themselves in their previous shows. For the first time, the songs advanced the story instead of interrupting it, with no pointless chorus blow-outs or specialty numbers to distract from the forward motion of the plot.

Also of note was the use of choreographer Agnes deMille's dances (with a huge assist to her arranger, Trude Rittman). The great deMille's contributions were highlighted by the first-act ballet "Laurey Makes Up Her Mind," in which the amorous subconscious desires of our conflicted heroine Laurey are danced out as a part of the story and not as a throwaway fantasy. The effect of *Oklahoma!* on the art form simply cannot be over-stated.

10. *CABARET* (1966)

Once again, director Harold Prince marshaled his for-midable forces to create a new, thrilling type of musical theater. Christopher Isherwood's *Berlin Stories* was adapted by John van Druten into the play *I am a Cam-era*, from which Joe Masteroff, John Kander, and Fred Ebb created the musical play *Cabaret*. The musical be-came a fascinating close-up study of passion and prej-udice played against the impending onslaught of Nazism.

Cabaret's freshness was in its structure. Three love plots of varying intensity were played in "real life" as conventional book musical scenes and numbers, with thrilling contrasting scenes taking place on the stage of the Kit Kat Klub, the cabaret where heroine Sally Bowles works. As embodied by the Emcee, a rouged-up, death's-head-looking evil clown, these scenes serve as ironic counterpoint to the action in the "book plot" preceding them, as in the number "Two Ladies," in which the Emcee and two girls describe their ideal live-in relationship just after Sally Bowles and her friend

Cliff Bradshaw (the Isherwood stand-in) have agreed to their own posslq'd relationship.

Adding to the brilliance of the enterprise was the work of Prince's set designer of choice, Boris Aronson, who provided his own stroke of brilliance by greeting the audience with a warped mirror hanging in front of the Broadhurst Theater stage, distoring the features of everything it reflected, including the audience. This chilling allegorical flourish was the preamble to a thrilling musical, worthy of its place in the canon.

Sunrise, Sunset

10 of New York's Longest-Running Musicals

Musical theater is a tricky business. Most shows never even see an opening night, let alone a New York run of any kind. But here are ten musicals that stayed around through many, many sunrises and sunsets.

1. ***THE FANTASTICKS***

This exquisite off-Broadway gem is the longest continuous run of formal (and probably informal) record in the history of American theater. A small (cast of eight, piano, and harp) adaptation of Rostand's play *Les Romanesques*, which took up residence in the tiny Sullivan Street Playhouse in Greenwich Village, it opened to good reviews and, well, just stayed around. For *forty-two years!* So ubiquitous was *The Fantasticks* on the New York theater scene that its corner of Sullivan Street was renamed *Fantasticks* Boulevard, and somewhere in mid-run (ha!), *New Yorker* magazine just started printing the number of performances "so far."

2. ***CATS***

Cats opened on Broadway on October 7, 1982. When it closed on September 10, 2000, it reigned as the longest-running Broadway show ever. The best way to explain the worldwide success of Andrew Lloyd Webber and T. S. Eliot's *Cats*, as a show and as a marketing phenomenon, is the faith in a pure form of theatrical magic. *Cats* is about as deep and heavy as a child's wading pool, but show fans, casual theatergoers, and ordinary folk all ate it up. The type of mega-hit that sustains the Broadway tourist industry for decades, *Cats* rode high from the first glimpse of the trademark green cat's eyes, and 7485 performances and nearly eighteen years later, the kitties left the Broadway junkyard for good.

3. *A CHORUS LINE*

Director-choreographer Michael Bennett's supreme achievement from 1975 changed the way musicals were created and was the single most important musical of the 1970s. The workshop atmosphere in which the show was created gave it the very collaborative aura necessary to ensure the show's success.

A very fictionalized audition for a spot on the chorus line in a Broadway show (no director-choreographer at the time would have cared to know "a little something about" his dancers), its theme—people literally putting themselves "on the line" for acceptance—was so universally embraced that the show became a nearly unprecedented phenomenon, with the famous fighting of the great unwashed for tickets as soon as the show opened downtown at the Public Theater. And when it moved uptown to Broadway's Shubert Theater, you couldn't find a ticket for love or money. For years, *A Chorus Line* was Broadway's evergreen seventies phenomenon. Upon passing *Grease* as the longest-running Broadway show ever, performance number 3,389 was greeted with hysteria bordering on anarchy. *A Chorus Line* finally closed in 1990, after 6,137 performances.

4. *THE PHANTOM OF THE OPERA*

The biggest commercial hit in Broadway history, *The Phantom of the Opera* was a monster hit in London, and, as soon as casting snafus were untangled, was a pre-sold hit by the time it opened on Broadway in January of 1988. Andrew Lloyd Webber's lush musical treatment of Gaston Leroux's Gothic horror tale played smartly to the romantic notions inherent in the story and yielded some gorgeous music, including the Phantom's haunting "The Music of the Night," heroine Christine's elegy for her father, "Wishing You Were Somehow Here Again," and the clever Puccini pastiche of "Prima Donna."

The book and lyrics (by Charles Hart and Richard Stilgoe) were not up to the level of Lloyd Webber's music, but the brilliant scenery and costumes of Maria Bjornson, and Harold Prince's masterful direction, gave the eye much to take in, and the presence of the Phantom, commanding in a deceptively small role, has assured the show's long-running success. Oh, and that Phantom mask logo sells a LOT of T-shirts and key chains.

5. *LES MISÉRABLES*

The recently-closed *Les Misérables* was a profiteer of the 1980s Brit-popera phenomenon. About as non-American a musical as you could create, *Les Miz* began life as a French (really? *Wow!*) pop spectacle, adapted from the Victor Hugo novel, which attracted the attention of London's Royal Shakespeare Company. The superb RSC staging, by Trevor Nunn and John Caird, was picked up for a commercial run by eight-hundred-pound gorilla Cameron Mackintosh, and it is still running in London today.

Broadway audiences clamored for the next big thing (especially since the last two Tony winners had been the not-hot, not-sexy, not-foreign *Big River* and *The Mystery of Edwin Drood*), and *Les Miz* set a single-day ticket record when the box office opened in January 1987, and rode high for years as the Broadway engagement settled in, and folks who missed it on tour made a New York field trip to see it.

Interestingly enough, deep into the run, the show's production team canned its entire Broadway cast and retooled the show considerably, citing a terrible staleness to the proceedings. Most long-running shows do attempt to "freshen up" from time to time, but *Les Misérables*, in performing a major overhaul on cast and script, went the extra yard and, as a result, ran an extra six years.

6. *OKLAHOMA!*

The first super-hit musical, and rightly so, Rodgers and Hammerstein's *Oklahoma!* was a cultural phenomenon that changed the way the Broadway game was played. *Oklahoma!*'s wartime success, unprecedented for any musical, forced Broadway audiences literally at gunpoint to accept and embrace the Rodgers and Hammerstein concept of the integrated musical play and abandon the crudely constructed musical comedies that filled Broadway before it.

Oklahoma!'s startlingly original stagecraft was wedded to what Oscar Hammerstein called a "heartiness" and a simplicity of message that wartime audiences craved. Word-of-mouth built, as it does with all hits, and *Oklahoma!* became a template for all the Broadway musicals that followed, both onstage and, thanks to the business acumen of producer Theresa Helburn's Theater Guild, offstage as well.

7. *NUNSENSE*

Teeny-tiny seems to be the way to succeed off-Broadway. Like *The Fantasticks* before it, *Nunsense* is a very small show with a very simple premise. Also like *The Fantasticks*, *Nunsense* creator Dan Goggin probably owns a small island by now. By the time it closed it had racked up 3,672 perfromances and spawned countless sequels (including an all-male version, *Nunsense A-Men!)*

Goggins's show—about a small group of nuns (from, uh, Mt. Saint Helen's School) holding a talent show to raise money—is totally tongue in cheek, yet not really blasphemous (unless an occasional PG curse word knocks your lights out) or disrespectful, and a fairly innocuous evening. Religious groups have obviously gotten a huge kick out of it, and lay folk must get a charge out of seeing roller-skating, ventriloquist nuns as well.

8. *GREASE*

Yet another "little musical that could," Jim Jacobs and Warren Casey's tale of better living and loving through doo-wop ran for over eight years, ending its run in 1980 as the all-time long-running champ, with 3,388 performances. From inauspicious beginnings at Chicago's dingy Kingston Mines club to the heights of Broadway is a strange journey.

Grease is notable not only for its long run and the inexplicably popular film version, but it also had a monstrously successful revival in 1994, with many non-Broadway performers like Brooke Shields, Maureen McCormick, Mickey Dolenz, and Jon Secada slipping into and out of the not-exactly-Shakespearean roles of hot-rod guys, good girls, and Pink Ladies.

9. *MY FAIR LADY*

My Fair Lady's success came at a time when America was on top of the world, and Broadway shows were very chic. The biggest hit of the 1950's, *My Fair Lady* was what the pundits called a "snob hit," but without the snobbery. A revival of Shaw's *Pygmalion* might have received polite nods of approval, but a musical version adapted by Lerner and Loewe? Starring Julie Andrews? Cha-*ching!*

Like *Oklahoma!* and *South Pacific* before it, *My Fair Lady* was a status symbol show, one that people arranged their lives around in an effort to see. The presence of the *My Fair Lady* cast album in one's den gave one social Brownie points, and well, dear, if you had tickets, would you like to run for PTA president?

10. *FIDDLER ON THE ROOF*

Fiddler on the Roof surpassed *Hello, Dolly!* to become the all-time longest running musical in Broadway history (not surpassed until *Grease*, many years later). Many elements, not the least of which was its quality, combined to make it a 3,242-performance success.

Fiddler was produced by Hal Prince, staged by Jerome Robbins, with score by Jerry Bock and Sheldon Harnick and book by Joseph Stein. It starred Zero Mostel. Mercy! But as brilliantly crafted a show as it is, Tevye and his daughters ran forever for two big reasons. One reason was the success with the theater party business, which caters to large ticket-buying groups, many of which are Jewish and play right into the hands of a Jewish-themed show like *Fiddler*. The other, larger reason was the warm-hearted universality of the show, which was embodied by its magnificent opening number, "Tradition," which placed the Russian-Jewish village of Anatevka firmly in the Neighborhood of Man. Such loving care assured that the show would play in Oslo, Tokyo, and Buenos Aires as well as Broadway's Imperial Theater.

Index

About the Author

Tom Shea is an accomplished singer and actor and has appeared in *The Golden Apple*, *Lady In the Dark*, *One Touch of Venus*, *Knickerbocker Holiday*, *Utopia, Ltd.*, and *The Grand Duke*. He has written for The Baseball Workshop, Total Sports, and Total Baseball. He lives in Chicago with his cat, Macheath. This is his first book.